MISSION COLLEGE
LEARNING RESOURCE SERVICES

D0149232

3 1215 00049 1230

# VIOLETS
### AND
# VINEGAR

Beyond Bartlett,
Quotations By
and About
Women

# JILLY
# COOPER
### AND
# TOM
# HARTMAN

9-12-83
7275928

# VIOLETS
### AND
# VINEGAR

### Beyond Bartlett,
Quotations By
and About
## Women

# JILLY
# COOPER
### AND
# TOM
# HARTMAN

𝔰𝔡
**STEIN AND DAY/*Publishers*/New York**

First published in the United States of America in 1982
This edition and selection copyright © 1980 by Jillv Cooper and Tom Hartman
All rights reserved
Printed in the United States of America
Stein and Day/*Publishers*/Scarborough House
Briarcliff Manor, New York 10510


*Library of Congress Cataloging in Publication Data*

Cooper, Jilly.
    Violets and vinegar.

    Includes index.
        1. Quotations, English.        2. Women—Quotations.
3. English literature—Women authors.        I. Hartman,
Tom, 1935–        II. Title.
PN6081.5.C58  1982        082        80-9059
ISBN 0-8128-2813-5                        AACR2

Ref
PN
6081.5
.C58
1982

FOR WENDY WITH LOVE

**Authors' Note**
Many people have offered us their help and
advice. In particular we would like to thank
Miss Barbara Cooper, Mr Jeremy Carlos-
Clarke, Mrs Felix Stone, Miss Maxine Green
and Mrs Beryl Hill. We are also deeply grateful
to all those who have given us permission to
include copyright material. Their names are to
be found in the list of acknowledgements
towards the end of the book. While every
attempt has been made to trace the owners of
all copyright matter reprinted in this book,
some will inevitably have slipped through the
net. We hope that they will get in touch with
us, so that suitable acknowledgement may be
made in future editions.

*Jilly Cooper*

*Tom Hartman*

# Contents

# VIOLETS
### AND
# VINEGAR
Beyond Bartlett,
Quotations By
and About
Women

# JILLY
# COOPER
### AND
# TOM
# HARTMAN.

# Introduction

When something gives you pleasure, you want not only to share the moment, but to record it. Tom Hartman, my co-editor, and I have been friends for many years. We are both compulsive readers, and have for a long time been swapping quotations and overheard remarks that have appealed to us, and marking in books passages we have particularly enjoyed.

Some time ago it occurred to us that in most anthologies and dictionaries of quotations the contributors have been at least ninety per cent male. This would have been understandable in anthologies of painting, or music, or sculpture, for there have been few great women painters, or composers, or – excepting Elizabeth Frink – great sculptors. Literature, however, is different. It is the only intellectual field to which women over the centuries have made an indispensable contribution. In fact, it would be true to say that since the war most of the major novels have been written by women. It seemed to us unfair that anthologies of both poetry and prose should be so male-dominated; we therefore decided to produce one that was composed entirely of the work of women writers.

When we started selecting material, my husband was extremely nervous that he would be caught in the cross-fire if Tom and I quarrelled over something one or the other disliked or insisted on including. In fact we never had a cross word. Our tastes turned out to be complementary and surprisingly similar. Whenever we wanted to include a quotation the other wasn't wild about, we justified our choice by claiming it came from a *seminal* work!

My own problem, as with everything else, was excess. I could happily have filled an entire book with Jane Austen, Stevie Smith, E. M. Delafield and one or two of my favourite modern novelists, such as Barbara Pym and Elizabeth Taylor. Tom, therefore, as well as providing at least fifty per cent of the material, had to prune my own contributions vigorously, and on occasions quietly mislaid things I wanted to put in, but which he disliked intensely. One of his *bêtes noires* was Edith Sitwell, and I had to keep on retrieving her crumpled-up poems from the waste-paper basket. Nor could he stand E. M. Delafield. This was ancient prejudice, because the high-handed Lady Boxe, one of the characters pilloried in her *Diary of a Provincial Lady,* was based on a friend of his aunt. The fact that I have been unable to overcome some of his other prejudices will be apparent from the biographical index at the end of the book, which is all his work. The reader will therefore appreciate that this is a very personal anthology.

Our principles of selection were as follows. We did not deliberately omit things because they were well known, but we hope that many of the quotations will be new to the reader. We have only chosen material which seemed to us either beautiful or illuminating, or particularly well written, or which highlights a turning-point in history, or because it made us laugh. Part of the charm of many women writers is their preposterousness, their extravagance, their gusto, and their ability to write something so frightful as to be funny.

We are aware, of course, of notable omissions. I am still kicking myself for not remembering the name of the actress who said: 'I like to wake up every morning feeling a new man.'

We are well aware that the extreme fringes of Women's Lib are not represented. Nor have we allowed ourselves to be seduced into including obscure works by modern poets, simply because other people less philistine than us claim to understand them. Hence no Sylvia Plath or Elizabeth Bishop.

Some authors too are much easier to quote from than others, and sadly, for this reason, many distinguished writers – Susan Hill, Elizabeth Jane Howard, Alison Lurie, Iris Murdoch, Somerville and Ross – have been left out or are little represented. This was not because we do not admire them, nor because we haven't read their books, but simply because their genius is cumulative. They build up their effect by a host of little details co-ordinated into a total mood. They do not yield up the detached metaphor, nor the sparkling epigram.

Having said this, I think what surprised and delighted us was how very good women writers are. Their canvas may be smaller, but their workmanship is often more exquisite. Apart too from Dorothy Parker, Nancy Mitford, the solecisms of Margot Asquith and the occasional spiky retort from Lady Astor, women on the whole have not got a reputation for being great wits. But we found that Margaret

Halsey, Helen Rowland and Mary Wilson Little hold their own as epigrammatists in any field.

Having dealt with selection, we now turn to order. According to Lady Troubridge (not the one who had the dubious distinction of having carried on a rip-roaring affair with Radclyffe Hall, but the Lady T.who wrote one of the most widely read books on etiquette of the twentieth century), 'The correct introduction does not consist merely in making two strangers known to one another. One should try to create an immediate friendship between people who are meeting for the first time, and to assist smooth and pleasant conversation.' So, in order to give the book some shape, we have divided it into twenty-four sections, each of which is prefaced by a brief introduction. But it will soon be appreciated by the reader that these sections are somewhat artificial in that many of the passages quoted would fit as well under any of half a dozen headings. Occasionally we have interjected brief remarks about the authors when we felt that they would amuse or lend poignancy to a quotation, but on the whole biographical information is confined to the index at the back of the book.

Finally, Lady Troubridge stresses that the most important purpose of an introduction is to make strangers wish to continue the acquaintance. This is also our hope. If readers who enjoy a few lines of Pamela Hansford Johnson or a fragment of Martha Gellhorn feel their appetites sufficiently whetted to seek out the original book, then our task will have been well rewarded.

*Jilly Cooper*

# I Liked You Better Smaller

It cannot be denied that a disproportionately large number of great women writers have been childless. One has only to think of Jane Austen, the Brontës, Dorothy Wordsworth, George Eliot, Fanny Burney, Christina Rossetti, Emily Dickinson, Virginia Woolf, Katherine Mansfield, Dorothy Parker, Nancy Mitford, Iris Murdoch, Barbara Pym – to name but a few. It is impossible to say whether these ladies wrote to compensate for being childless, and often husbandless, or whether it is that a woman whose creative ambitions are focused on motherhood does not have the urge to write. It could simply be that looking after children is such a draining, distracting experience that one has no energy to write – a case of the play-pen being mightier than the typewriter.

If Elizabeth Barrett Browning, herself childless, had been writing today she would probably have been clobbered by the sexual equality act for pointing out that only women know the knack of tying sashes, fitting baby-shoes, and stringing together pretty words that make *no* sense. Certainly it is much easier to string together pretty words that *make sense* when children are not around. It is impossible to write if one is woken up six times a night by a howling baby, or constantly interrupted by a cavalcade from Porlock demanding glasses of Ribena, elastic bands for pony tails, and plaster to put on non-existent cuts. It may be that childbirth saps a writer's creative energy, but it is certain that a full-time mother and a great writer is a rare combination.

It is interesting in this section to observe how past and present writers differ in their attitude both to parents and to children. The Victorians, whatever their dark private thoughts, honoured their fathers and mothers in public, and regarded their offspring as innocent rosy-cheeked angels. There is a world of difference between the reverence Queen Victoria is trying to instil into her children on page 23 and the profound contempt felt for her own mother by Mrs Robert Henrey's Paloma on page 21. The Victorians would have been horrified by the touching voluptuous delight Nell Dunn's Poor Cow takes in her small boy when he disturbs her much-needed sleep with icy feet and a runny nose. They would also have been shocked by Nancy Mitford's description of a new-born baby as 'a howling orange in a black wig'. Nor would they ever have stooped to Elizabeth Taylor's realism (page 19) in depicting an older man's revulsion when his grandchild's nappies are changed in the drawing-room.

Perhaps Victorian women writers didn't go in for realism because they were protected by armies of nannies and nursery-maids from the more unsalubrious aspects of bringing up children. But Gwen Raverat points out (on page 24) that although children didn't see so much of their mothers in those days, it doesn't appear to have affected the love they felt for them. It is interesting that Juliet Mitchell, writing about children on a kibbutz, seems to agree that children fare better when they grow up out of the constant searchlight of parental love and anxiety. Margaret Lane, however, clearly finds the isolated regimentation of Beatrix Potter's childhood unnatural and unkind.

One thing that did move nineteenth century writers was poverty, particularly its effect on children, a subject to which, today, shored up by the great featherbed of the welfare state, we have become almost indifferent. There is a moving contrast between the London poor described by Dinah Mulock and Flora Thompson's merry, roistering country children on their way to school.

We conclude this section with Dorothea Eastwood's poem 'To my Son', because it expresses the universal truth that, however much pain you undergo giving birth to a child, and however much you may love and protect him, in the end he will have to face the world alone.


No test tube can breed love and affection. No frozen packet of semen ever read a story to a sleepy child.

**Shirley Williams,** DAILY MIRROR, 2 March 1978


Be kind to thy father, for when thou wert young,
    Who loved thee so fondly as he?
He caught the first accents that fell from thy tongue,
    And joined in thy innocent glee.

**Margaret Courtney,** 'BE KIND'


Observers of collective methods of child-rearing in the kibbutzim in Israel note that the child who is reared by a trained nurse . . . does not suffer the backwash of typical parental anxieties and thus may positively gain by the system.

**Juliet Mitchell,** WOMEN'S ESTATE


No man is responsible for his father. That is entirely his mother's affair.

**Margaret Turnbull,** ALABASTER LAMPS


'Who was your mother?'
    'Never had none!' said the child with another grin.
'Never had any mother? What do you mean? Where were you born?'
    'Never was born!' persisted Topsy.

**Harriet Beecher Stowe,** UNCLE TOM'S CABIN


Then there were his pants. She thought about his little cotton-knit drawers, two-and-eleven in Woolworth's with blue dogs running riot all over them. And his best jumper – she had bought it in a jumble sale on Clapham Common. It was burgundy-and-pink stripes, with short sleeves, and his little white neck stuck like a stalk out of the top, his black hair hanging in silky scoops over the back. She thought about this and about how he woke her in the morning, putting his face very close to hers and saying, 'Mum, Mum, I wanna see Mama.' And then, if she tried to go on sleeping, tried desperately to cling to the world of warm dreams, he would climb on her head, sit down and bounce about, or gently touch each eye and say, 'Mum open eye', putting his small mouth and often runny nose close against hers. Till finally she opened the covers and dragged him in with her and held him tight up against her, warming his cold feet between her legs. And then she felt an overpowering love for him – a love which didn't seem to have a beginning or an end. They would spit Spangles into each other's mouths as they lay in bed in the mornings, listening to the small, throbbing transistor.

**Nell Dunn,** POOR COW


Flora sat on the sofa. Alice was on her lap, having her napkin changed.

Good God, thought Percy.

Flora clasped the little feet together in one hand and lifted the bright red bottom from the steaming napkins, saying 'How nice to see you Grandpa. Do sit down, Percy dear. Wherever you'll be most comfortable.'

'I've just called in on Richard,' Percy said, taking a chair by the fire and keeping his eyes away from the baby. *In the drawing room,* he thought. *In company.*

Flora gave a little sigh in her mind; the only place where she *could* give it . . . She began to dredge Alice with powder. Then she pinned her into clean napkins and handed her to her grandfather. She went out with the wet napkins and left Percy with Patrick. A long string of dribble swayed from Alice's mouth and attached itself to his shoulder. Her head bobbed uncertainly on it's frail neck. He was afraid that she might nod it right off. Some talcum powder came off her legs on to his sleeve. With both hands needed to hold her, he could not protect himself. He kept his head back, rigid, as far from her as he could, but her face came nearer and nearer and with a sudden lurch she fell forward, her wet, open mouth pressed slobbering against his chin.

'Shall I take her, sir?' Patrick asked.

In spite of his relief, Percy resented the 'Sir'. A dozen years younger than me at most, he thought sourly, and wildly inaccurately, as he brushed and mopped himself.

**Elizabeth Taylor,** THE SOUL OF KINDNESS


A man finds out what is meant by a spitting image when he tries to feed cereal to his infant.

**Imogene Fey**

Women know
    The way to rear up children (to be just),
They know the simple, merry, tender, knack
    Of tying sashes, fitting baby-shoes,
And stringing pretty words that make no sense.

**Elizabeth Barrett Browning,** AURORA LEIGH*


She was provided with a Scottish nurse of Calvinistic principles; she had a clean starched piqué frock every morning and 'cotton stockings striped round and round like a zebra's legs'; a cutlet and rice pudding came up the back stairs every day for lunch, and in the afternoon, unless it rained, McKenzie the nurse took her for a good walk. What more could a child want?

**Margaret Lane,** THE TALE OF BEATRIX POTTER


I know I was cruel to other children because I remember stuffing their nostrils with putty, and beating a little boy with stinging nettles.

**Vita Sackville-West,** quoted in PORTRAIT OF
A MARRIAGE by Nigel Nicolson


The fussed shall be last, and the last shall be fussed.

**Lady Jekyll**


No one ever pruned me. If you have been sunned through and through like an apricot on a wall from your earliest days, you are oversensitive to any withdrawal of heat.

**Margot Asquith,** AUTOBIOGRAPHY


Children sleep either alone or with small toy animals. The wisdom of such behaviour is unquestionable, as it frees them from the immeasurable tedium of being privy to the whispered confessions of others. I have yet to come across a teddy bear who was harboring the secret desire to wear a maid's uniform.

**Fran Lebowitz,** METROPOLITAN LIFE

---

*(Elizabeth Barrett Browning) was just like a King Charles spaniel, the same large soft brown eyes, the full silky curls falling round her face like a spaniel's ears, the same pathetic wistfulness of expression. Her mouth was too large for beauty, but full of eloquent curves and movements. Her voice was very expressive, her manner gentle but full of energy. At time she became intense in tone and gesture, but it was so spontaneous that nobody could ever have thought it assumed as is the fashion with later poets and poetesses.

**Mrs David Ogilvy,**
RECOLLECTIONS OF MRS BROWNING

My mother never did like me, and she didn't even hide it. She said I was ugly and silly. My hair was too straight, my legs were too long and thin, my neck was scraggy as a chicken's . . . fool that she was! That neck she thought scraggy was responsible for my biggest successes! I tell you, my rat, in order to get on in life one must not remain a child too long. I hated being a child. One must leave one's parents early, especially one's mother. Mothers are never any good for their daughters. They forget they were just as ugly and silly and scraggy as little girls. They only tell you about their years of success, the years when they met your father. What a to-do catching one man and bragging about it during an entire lifetime!

**Mrs Robert Henrey,** Paloma

To be sure a stepmother to a girl is a different thing to a second wife to a man.

**Mrs Gaskell,** Wives and Daughters

Before he left, Aunt William pressed a sovereign into his hand, as if it were conscience money. He, on his side, took it as though it were a doctor's fee, and both ignored the transaction.

**Ada Leverson,** The Twelfth Hour

Mr Evans gave her advice, too, on how to bring up her five childen. The young Flindts, he stipulated, must be sent to bed early so as to rise early. They must never be allowed to indulge in that bad habit of day-dreaming in bed at any time whatsoever; most particularly before getting up. As soon as their heads touched the pillow, they must compose themselves obediently to instantaneous sleep. As soon as they woke, they must spring energetically out of bed, ready to face what the day might bring. To doze comfortably on and off, to build dream castles in the air in that delicious interval between waking and rising, to count either flies on the ceiling or innocent white sheep jumping over a stile, was detrimental to the young.

**Bea Howe,** Child in Chile

Though she lacked imagination, Brenda would go to any lengths rather than cause herself embarrassment. It was her upbringing. As a child she had been taught it was rude to say no unless she didn't mean it. If she was offered another piece of cake and she wanted it she was obliged to refuse out of politeness. And if she didn't want it she had to say yes, even if it choked her.

**Beryl Bainbridge,** The Bottle Factory Outing

21

So long as little children are allowed to suffer, there is no true love in this world.

Isadora Duncan

No one, whose sole experience in the baby-line lies among the well-fed, well-clothed, well-tended offspring of the respectable classes, can see without pain the vast differences between them and 'poor people's babies'. Especially the London poor. Their pinched faces; their thin flaccid limbs, shivering under the smallest possible covering of threadbare flannel and worn-out calico; their withered, old-like expression, so different from the round-eyed, apple-cheeked simplicity that well-to-do parents love – no wonder it was rather hard to keep in healthy, satisfied quietness poor people's babies. Babies, too, who from morning till night seldom or never know what it is to cuddle in warmly to the natural nest – the mother's own bosom.

Dinah Maria Mulock, POOR PEOPLE'S CHILDREN

School began at nine o'clock, but the hamlet children set out on their mile-and-a-half walk there as soon as possible after their seven o'clock breakfast, partly because they liked plenty of time to play on the road and partly because their mothers wanted them out of the way before house-cleaning began . . .

They were strong lusty children, let loose from control, and there was plenty of shouting, quarrelling and often fighting among them. In more peaceful moments they would squat in the dust of the road and play marbles, or sit on a stone heap and play dibs with pebbles, or climb into the hedges after birds' nests or blackberries, or to pull long trails of bryony to wreathe round their hats. In winter they would slide on the ice on the puddles, or make snowballs – soft ones for their friends, and hard ones with a stone inside for their enemies.

After the first mile or so the dinner baskets would be raided; or they would creep through the bars of the padlocked field gates for turnips to pare with the teeth and munch, or for handfuls of green pea shucks, or ears of wheat, to rub out the sweet, milky grain between the hands and devour. In spring they ate the young green from the hawthorn hedges, which they called 'bread and cheese', and sorrel leaves from the wayside, which they called 'sour grass', and in the autumn there was an abundance of haws and blackberries and sloes and crab-apples for them to feast upon. There was always something to eat, and they ate, not so much because they were hungry, as from habit and relish of the wild food.

Flora Thompson, LARK RISE TO CANDLEFORD

How pleasant is Saturday night,
   When I've tried all the week to be good,
And not spoke a word that was bad,
   And obliged everyone that I could.

Tomorrow our holy day comes,
   Which our merciful Father has given,
That we may rest from our work,
   And prepare for His beautiful heaven.

**Nancy Sproat** 'Saturday Night'

The golf links lie so near the mill
   That almost every day
The labouring children can look out
   And watch the men at play.

**Sarah Norcliffe Cleghorn,** 'Quatrain'

Cleaning your house while your kids are still growing is like shovelling the walk before it stops snowing.

**Phyllis Diller**

*None* of you can *ever* be proud enough of being the *child* of SUCH a Father who has not his *equal* in this world – so great, so good, so faultless. Try, all of you, to follow in his footsteps and don't be discouraged, for to be *really* in everything like him *none* of you, I am sure, will ever be. Try, therefore, to be like him in *some* points, and you will have *acquired a great deal.*

**Queen Victoria,** letter to the Prince of Wales,
26 August 1857

I'm sorry you are wiser,
   I'm sorry you are taller;
I liked you better foolish
   And I liked you better smaller.

**Aline Kilmer,** 'For the Birthday of a Middle-
Aged Child'

Perhaps the best function of parenthood is to teach the young creature to love with *safety,* so that it may be able to venture unafraid when later emotion comes; the thwarting of the instinct to love is the root of all sorrow and not sex only but divinity itself is insulted when it is repressed. To disapprove, to condemn – the human soul shrivels under barren righteousness.

**Freya Stark,** TRAVELLER'S PRELUDE

I can never remember being bathed by my mother, or ever having my hair brushed by her, and I should not have liked it if she had done anything of the kind. We did not feel it was her place to do such things; though my father used to cut our finger-nails with his sharp white-handled knife, and that we felt quite pleasant and proper. Anyhow there was no need for my mother to do such things, for Nana hardly ever went out, and if she did the housemaid or the nursery maid was left in charge of us. About once in two years or three years, there was an appalling crisis because Nana left us poor little orphans, while she went away for a week's holiday; but it was all arranged beforehand, and my mother did nothing extra herself, except perhaps a little more *telling* than usual.

**Gwen Raverat,** PERIOD PIECE

Oliver's temperature zig-zagged across the chart, so that he could not be allowed home the next day.

'Really, Mrs Davenant!' said a stout and exasperated woman, who was the almoner, 'your child is not the only one in the hospital.'

'He is the only child of mine in the hospital,' said Julia.

**Elizabeth Taylor,** AT MRS LIPPINCOTE'S

Now listen, Christopher, you must not cry darling – just because a lady kicks you . . . You mustn't cry . . . Because in one way or another everybody gets kicked . . . Certainly – we all get kicked. Daddy gets kicked and he doesn't cry . . . No – I don't kick him . . . But somebody else may.

**Ruth Draper,** THE CHILDREN'S PARTY

Son, I am powerless to protect you though
My heart for yours beats ever anxiously,
Blind through piteous darkness you must go,
And find with a new vision lights I see.
If it might ease you I would bear again
All the old suffering that I too have known,
All sickness, terror, and the spirit's pain,
But you, alas, must make those three your own.
Yes, though I beat away a thousand fears
And forge your armour without flaw or chink,
And though I batter Heaven with my prayers,
Yet from a self-filled cup of grief you drink.
Oh, son of woman, since I gave you breath
You walk alone through life to face your death.

**Dorothea Eastwood, 'To My Son'**

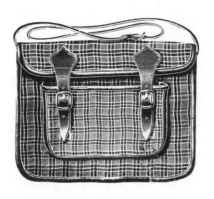

# What Is This Education?

The education of women is a comparatively new phenomenon. 'Be good sweet maid, and let who can be clever,' said Charles Kingsley, while Hannah More believed that the poor should be undereducated to keep them in their place. Lady Bradshaw felt the same about girls: 'I hate', she wrote to Samuel Richardson, 'to see Latin coming out of a woman's mouth.' In Dorita Fairlie Bruce's pre-war school, it was not at all the done thing to try hard at lessons (page 32), and even today there lingers a feeling that education doesn't matter so much for girls as for boys.

But, whatever the education buffs may have thought, there is no doubt that parents would never have got their daughters to boarding-school so willingly if it hadn't been for the marvellous publicity those establishments received from Angela Brazil and Enid Blyton. Millions of girls steeped themselves in *Claudine at St Clair's* and the *Malory Towers* books (particularly the passage on page 31), dreaming of instant popularity, of high jinks in the dorm, and of winning the lasting admiration of the dignified, grey-eyed head girl. So, from the age of ten onwards, well Brazilled and Blytoned girls started bullying their parents to send them away to school. The exciting vision created by the novelist was seldom, however, borne out in reality. I can never forget the isolation, the ruthless suppression of individuality, the yells of 'butterfingers' when one dropped a lacrosse ball, or the corrosive homesickness so brilliantly evoked by Gwen Raverat on page 32. Equally stultifying was the heartiness and the deliberate rejection of glamour. On page 30 Viva King shows how prudish nuns could be. The girls themselves were almost as bad. Their attitude, according to E. Arnot Robertson, who went to Sherborne, was:

'Oh goody, goody, we ought to do well in lacrosse this term. Hooray for the House, and I'm glad I'm not pretty.'

But day-dreaming still continued, as F. Tennyson Jesse suggests on page 31 in the not altogether characteristic quotation from her brilliant book *The Lacquer Lady*, which has recently been reissued. Occasionally even in Angela Brazil lust was allowed to raise its ugly head (page 32).

Discipline must come through liberty. Here is a great principle which it is difficult for followers of the common-school methods to understand. How shall one obtain discipline in a class of free children? Certainly in our system we have a concept of discipline very different from that commonly accepted. If discipline is founded upon liberty, the discipline itself must necessarily be *active*. We do not consider an individual disciplined only when he has been rendered as artificially silent as a mute and as immovable as a paralytic. He is an individual *annihilated,* not *disciplined.*

Maria Montessori, THE MONTESSORI METHOD


Whipping and abuse are like laudanum; you have to double the dose as the sensibilities decline.

Harriet Beecher Stowe, UNCLE TOM'S CABIN


Prejudices, it is well known, are most difficult to eradicate from the heart whose soil has never been loosened or fertilized by education; they grow there, firm as weeds among stones.

Charlotte Brontë, JANE EYRE


My plan of instruction is extremely simple and limited. They learn, on weekdays, such coarse works as may fit them for servants. I allow of no writing for the poor. My object is not to make fanatics, but to train up the lower classes in habits of industry and piety.

Hannah More to the Bishop of Bath and Wells, 1801


Education was almost always a matter of luck – usually ill-luck – in those distant days.

George Eliot, THE MILL ON THE FLOSS


The liberty of the child should have as its *limit* the collective interest; as its form, what we usually consider good breeding. We must therefore check in the child whatever offends or annoys others, or whatever tends towards rough or ill-bred acts. But all the rest – every manifestation having a useful scope, whatever it be, and under whatever form it expresses itself – must not only be permitted, but must be observed by the teacher.

Maria Montessori, THE MONTESSORI METHOD


Better build schoolrooms for 'the boy'
Than cells and gibbets for 'the man'.

Eliza Cook, A SONG FOR THE RAGGED SCHOOLS

Take Robin out. He eats several meals, and a good many sweets. He produces a friend, and we take both to Corfe Castle . . . Take the boys back to the hotel for dinner. Robin says, whilst the friend is out of hearing: 'It's been nice for us, taking out Williams, hasn't it?' Hastily express appreciation of this privilege.

**E. M. Delafield,** DIARY OF A PROVINCIAL LADY

In my early life, and probably even today, it is not sufficiently understood that a child's education should include at least a rudimentary grasp of religion, sex and money. Without a basic knowledge of these three primary facts in a normal being's life – subjects which stir the emotions, create events and opportunities, and if they do not wholly decide must greatly influence an individual's personality – no human being's education can have a safe foundation.

**Phyllis Bottome,** SEARCH FOR A SOUL

Queen Elizabeth's mind, said Ascham, seemed to be free from female weakness, and her power of application was like a man's . . . They began the day by reading the New Testament in Greek, and then passages from Sophocles, which Ascham had chosen not only for their beauty but because they contained ideas which he thought would strengthen her mind against misfortune. She spent hours translating works from one foreign language into another and conversing with Ascham on intellectual topics in all the languages in turn; her favourite study, however, was history. She liked to spend three hours a day reading it, and would study the same period in all the different books she could get hold of. Her handwriting was now of exquisite beauty.

**Elizabeth Jenkins,** ELIZABETH THE GREAT

For precocity some great price is always demanded sooner or later in life.

**Margaret Fuller Ossoli,** DIARY

*Uncle Matthew:* Education! I was always led to suppose that no educated person ever spoke of notepaper, and yet I hear poor Fanny asking Sadie for notepaper. What is this education? Fanny talks about mirrors and mantelpieces, handbags and perfume, she takes sugar in her coffee, has a tassel on her umbrella, and I have no doubt that if she is ever fortunate enough to catch a husband she will call his father and mother Father and Mother. Will the wonderful education she is getting make up to the unhappy brute for all these endless pinpricks? Fancy hearing one's wife talk about notepaper – the irritation!

**Nancy Mitford,** THE PURSUIT OF LOVE

'Then you're looking forward to going back to school?'
'I shall like the society of boys of my own sex again,' he said grandly.

Ada Leverson, LOVE AT SECOND SIGHT

As far as education went there is little to relate. The nuns at Hemelsdael were ignorant and their ethics odd; we were given good marks for telling on each other. I was very aware of the lack of colour and of the drabness which is part of the life of self-denial that nuns impose upon themselves. The very atmosphere in the convent seemed grey and there was an ever-present smell, as of the slates we wrote on. The food was horrid and I had to wrap in bread the lumps of slimy grey meat-loaf we were often given, before I could bring myself to swallow it, washed down with the compulsory sour beer. We wore grey flannel chemises when having an occasional bath. *'Pourquoi est-ce que je dois porter cette chemise, Madame?'* I asked, to receive the answer, *'Parce que l'ange gardien vous regarde.'* A nun would rush in to dry one under the clammy flannel as, at this stage especially, one might be tempted to take a risk with the guardian angel.

Viva King, THE WEEPING AND THE LAUGHTER

The only inequalities that matter begin in the mind. It is not income levels but differences in mental equipment that keep people apart, breed feelings of inferiority.

Jacquetta Hawkes, NEW STATESMAN, January 1957

I shall always have a strong preference for cheap books myself, even if they did not pay; all my little friends happen to be shilling people. I do dislike the modern fashion of giving children heaps of expensive things which they don't look at twice.

Beatrix Potter in a letter to Norman Warne, 1903

The difficulty in writing truthfully about parents is that the tone of criticism or the flavour of sentimentalism is bound to creep in. Parents are an excellent alibi: 'I might have done better if only my parents had understood me – brought me up more wisely – given me a more suitable education,' etc; though it is often to be found that another member of the family has turned out, notwithstanding all these obstacles, very well indeed. Devoted sons and daughters can also make an alibi of their devotion – so as to explain why they preferred to descend through history as examples of filial piety rather than do their job of work in the less appreciative outside world.

Phyllis Bottome, SEARCH FOR A SOUL

The three great stumbling-blocks in a girl's education, she says, are *homard à l'Americaine,* a boiled egg, and asparagus. Shoddy table manners, she says, have broken up many a happy home.

**Colette,** Gigi

Take Robin, now completely restored, back to school. I ask the Headmaster what he thinks of his progress. The Headmaster answers that the New Buildings will be finished before Easter, and that their numbers are increasing so rapidly that he will probably add on a New Wing next term, and perhaps I saw a letter of his in the *Times* replying to Dr Cecil Norwood? Make mental note to the effect that Headmasters are a race apart, and that if parents would remember this, much time could be saved.

**E. M. Delafield,** Diary of a Provincial Lady

'It's lovely to get that sudden view of it,' said Pamela, the quiet head-girl of North Tower, who had got into the coach just behind Alicia and Darrell. Her eyes shone as she spoke. 'I think Malory Towers shows at its best when we come to that corner, especially if the sun is behind it.'

Darrell could feel the warmth in Pamela's voice as she spoke of the school she loved. She looked at her and liked her.

Pamela saw her and laughed. 'You're just beginning at Malory Towers! You've got terms and terms before you. I'm just ending. Another term or two, and I shan't be coming to Malory Towers any more – except as an old girl. You make the most of it while you can.'

**Enid Blyton,** First Term at Malory Towers

The crocodile walked, as sedately as the blustering wind permitted, along the parade. A dark reptile, sharply articulated, it crawled along the strip of asphalt that separated the pearly wind-blown sky and pallid sea from the greys and duns of the town. To closer view it was plain that the reptile was divided into living sections; two and two the girls struggled along, beribboned sailor hats bent forward, brown kid-gloved hands clutching at the rims; heavily-swathed and many-looped dresses of blue serge blown against those moving pillars of flesh and bone that were never called legs, but referred to as lower limbs.

. . . and yet, beneath each stiff sailor hat was that sharp point of consciousness which is *I*, that in every one of them would persist inescapably for a lifetime . . . .

Each one was conscious, within the varying degree of her capacity for awareness, of the same physical sensations . . . I feel the wind and the heavy clothing and emptiness, my nose is cold, how good tea will be, even the thick chunks of bread and butter old Patterson gives us, and perhaps there will be potted meat, Lazenby's, I hope. And the ringletted, pretty, rather chinless Maude: Perhaps I shall get a few minutes talk with Miss Simpson . . . I can think of some excuse . . . I'd rather own up to something I haven't done – I can invent something – so that she scolds me, than not talk to her at all. It's rather thrilling being scolded by Miss Simpson, it makes me go sort of queer and trembly.

F. Tennyson Jesse, THE LACQUER LADY

School upset me very much at first, and I did not think that I could survive it, when the poison gas of homesickness settled down over my head, with its indescribable nausea. Though it was not really *home-sickness*, for I did not want to go home, only to escape into an air which I could breathe. I remember the first morning, kneeling at prayers . . . and staring out of the window, when my eyes ought to have been tight shut, and thinking: 'If only I could get out into that garden, perhaps I might feel better; anyhow there are some quite ordinary trees there, and some real grass' – for everything inside the house seemed to be tainted with a nightmare horror . . .

But the smell of the poison-gas never really went away, and I still now sometimes get a whiff of it when I have had to visit a school or stay with incongruous people. I must confess that once, when I was quite old and gone to call on some strangers, the alien feeling of the furniture became so appalling to me, after the maid had left me alone in the drawing-room, that I scrambled disgracefully out of the window and ran away down the drive and never returned. I can't imagine what the lady and the maid thought when they came in and found the room empty. Perhaps I have become their family ghost.

Gwen Raverat, PERIOD PIECE

I'm falling in love with her. I was taken with her, of course, the moment I saw her, but I believe now I'm going to have it badly. If there was a peach competition she'd win in a canter.

Angela Brazil, A HARUM SCARUM SCHOOLGIRL

Your work is always being held up as an example to them, and they know quite well it isn't sheer braininess, which can't be helped if you happen to be born that way. I wish for your own sake you'd slack off a bit, Nancy! It isn't done in the Lower Fifth, you know.

Dorita Fairlie Bruce, THAT BOARDING SCHOOL GIRL

With hair and girdles flying free,
The eager Forwards ran,
They seemed like rushing infantry,
Each one marked by an enemy,
In the opposing 'clan'.

**Thelma Hamilton Jones,** 'THE HOCKEY MATCH'


By the way, I hear Ruth's grandchildren are at that fashionable school in Dorset, and can already change wheels, top batteries and milk cows. They are going to learn to read next year, you say? At ten and twelve? Isn't that a little soon? One is afraid of over-exciting their brains. Still, if they want to learn, anything is better than repressing them.

**Rose Macaulay,** PERSONAL PLEASURES


'I incline to the theory that the plays of Shakespeare were written by Bacon.'

'How could they be?' said William . . . 'How could that man Ham__'

'I said Bacon.'

'Well, it's nearly the same . . . Well, if this man Bacon wrote them, they wouldn't put this man Shakespeare's name on the books . . .'

'Now, boys, I want you all please to listen to me . . . There was a man called Hamlet –'

'You just said he was called Bacon,' said William.

'I did *not* say he was called Bacon.'

'Yes, 'scuse me, you did . . . When I called him Ham, you said it was Bacon, and now you're calling him Ham yourself.'

'This was a different man . . . *Listen!* This man was called Hamlet and his uncle had killed his father because he wanted to marry his mother.'

'What did he want to marry his mother for?' said William. . .

'It was *Hamlet's* mother he wanted to marry.'

'Oh, that man what you think wrote the plays.'

'No, that was Bacon.'

'You said it was Ham a minute ago . . . I tell you what,' said William confidingly, 'let's say Eggs for both of them.'

**Richmal Crompton,** WILLIAM'S TREASURE TROVE

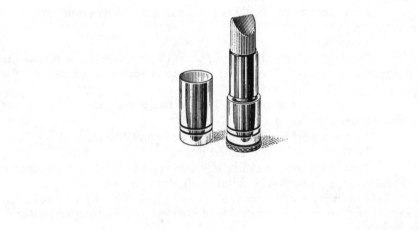

# Kiss Me and Be Quiet!

This section looks at love before marriage, at that restless, feverish period with all its aching joys and dizzy raptures when we are searching for someone to love. It is a time when the self-confident revel in the excitement of the chase; when the insecure and the lonely yearn for a permanent mate to settle down with. The very young girl is often confused by her own burgeoning sexuality. Enid Bagnold, having been a fat teenager, describes the wonder of suddenly discovering she was attractive. Simone de Beauvoir describes the ambivalence of the young girl's feelings: on the one hand, she wants to inflame men's passions, but having inflamed them she can't cope with the consequences and instinctively reaches for the fire bucket.

One of the salient characteristics of young love is its egoism. 'No one has been hurt like me,' cries the suffering victim, an illusion which Rose Macaulay neatly cuts down to size.

Men in the old days were supposed never to marry a fallen woman, which is why such a high price was put on virginity. This led to dislocated values, as Isak Dinesen points out (page 40); although Fran Lebowitz (page 36) gives another interpretation of the reasons for closely guarded virtue.

Before the second half of the twentieth century few women worked for a living, and most therefore depended on finding the right husband to support them for the rest of their lives. It is hardly surprising, therefore, that Madame de Staël wrote, several years before Byron, that love was a minor interest for men, but an all-consuming one for women. Byron's attitude was probably fortified by the fact that, attracting women so effortlessly, he probably didn't lose too many sleepless nights thinking about them.

Barbara Wilson shows that no woman comes between a man and his sporting activities (page 38). In a priceless extract from *The Rosary*, we see a young man falling for the Hon. Jane because she trounced him at golf (page 39), and finally the feline Seth, absolutely oozing animal magnetism, is outwitted by his prosaic cousin Flora in one of the funniest passages from *Cold Comfort Farm* (page 42).

A youth with his first cigar makes himself sick; a youth with his first girl makes other people sick.

**Mary Wilson Little**

A woman can look both moral and exciting – if she also looks as if it was quite a struggle.

**Edna Ferber,** READER'S DIGEST, December 1954

Tying her bonnet under her chin,
She tied her raven ringlets in;
But not alone in the silken snare
Did she catch her lovely floating hair,
For, tying her bonnet under her chin,
She tied a young man's heart within.

**Nora Perry,** 'THE LOVE-KNOT'


'Always be civil to the girls, you never know whom they may marry' is
an aphorism which has saved many an English spinster from being
treated like an Indian widow.

**Nancy Mitford,** LOVE IN A COLD CLIMATE


Stephon kissed me in the spring,
    Robin in the fall,
And Colin only looked at me
    And never kissed at all.

Stephon's kiss was lost in jest,
    Robin's lost in play,
But the kiss in Colin's eyes
    Haunts me night and day.

**Sara Teasdale,** 'THE LOOK'


Girls who put out are tramps. Girls who don't are ladies. This is,
however, a rather archaic usage of the word. Should one of you boys
happen upon a girl who doesn't put out, do not jump to the conclusion
that you have found a lady. What you have probably found is a lesbian.

**Fran Lebowitz,** METROPOLITAN LIFE


Though ash blonde she had, in some way, the personality more of a
dark woman. She was, in fact, the first blonde woman who had
attracted Thomas: for one thing, he had always detested pinkness, but
Anna had an opaque magnolia skin.

**Elizabeth Bowen,** THE DEATH OF THE HEART

Love's a disease. But curable . . . Did you ever look through a microscope at a drop of pond water? You see plenty of love there. All the amoebae getting married. I presume they think it very exciting and important. We don't.

Rose Macaulay, CREWE TRAIN

She is proud of catching male interest, of arousing admiration, but what revolts her is to be caught in return. With the coming of puberty she has become acquainted with shame; and the shame lingers on, mingled with her coquetry and her vanity. Men's stares flatter and hurt her simultaneously; she wants only what she shows to be seen: eyes are always too penetrating. Hence the inconsistency that men find disconcerting: she displays her *décolleté,* her legs, and when they are looked at she blushes, feels vexation. She enjoys inflaming the male, but if she sees that she has aroused his desire, she recoils in disgust. Masculine desire is as much an offence as it is a compliment; in so far as she feels herself responsible for her charm, or feels she is exerting it of her own accord, she is much pleased with her conquests but to the extent that her face, her figure, her flesh are facts she must bear with, she wants to hide them from this independent stranger who lusts after them.

Simone de Beauvoir, THE SECOND SEX

Let this great maxim be my virtue's guide –
In part she is to blame that has been tried:
He comes too near that comes to be denied.

Lady Mary Wortley Montagu, 'THE LADY'S RESOLVE'*

---

*Did I tell you Lady Mary Wortley is here? She laughs at my Lady Walpole, scolds my Lady Pomfret, and is laughed at by the whole town. Her dress, her avarice, and her imprudence must amaze anyone that never heard her name. She wears a foul mob that does not cover her greasy black locks, that hang loose, never combed or curled; an old mazarine blue wrapper, that gapes open and discovers a canvass petticoat. Her face swelled violently on one side with the remains of a __, partly covered with a plaister, and partly with white paint, which for cheapness she has bought so coarse that you would not use it to wash a chimney.

Letter from **Horace Walpole** to the Hon. H. S. Conway, 25 September 1740

Be plain in dress, and sober in your diet;
In short, my deary, kiss me, and be quiet.

> **Lady Mary Wortley Montagu, 'A SUMMARY OF LORD
> LYTTELTON'S ADVICE'**

From a wealth of living I have proved
I must be silent, if I would be loved.

> **Anna Wickham, 'THE AFFINITY'**

When you're married to someone they take you for granted, you're there, you're there to come home to, you're tied to the kitchen sink and when you go out, even if you look nice, they never say 'Oh you do look nice' or anything like that, and you sit in a corner all night and that's it. And he'll fuck off and talk to his mates. When you're living with someone it's fantastic. Everything that he does you do. They're so frightened of losing you they've got to keep you satisfied all the time.

> **Nell Dunn, POOR COW**

'It is a most repulsive quality, indeed,' said he. 'Often times very convenient, no doubt, but never pleasing. There is safety in reserve, but no attraction. One cannot love a reserved person.'

'Not till the reserve ceases towards oneself; and then the attraction may be the greater.'

> **Jane Austen, EMMA**

The Englishwoman is at the same time too little and too much detached from herself. A woman's supremacy in a man's life in England is precarious, she holds no security of tenure. Most probably she holds her property by the title-deeds of a pretty face – yet that superb confidence in herself which the Frenchwoman feels is never felt by the Englishwoman, who is on suffrance, always.

Once upon a time there was an Englishman who loved a woman madly, hopelessly, and for many months he besieged the citadel and never thought to win it. But at last she took pity on him and murmured, 'Yes – today. This afternoon.' In the twinkling of an eye his face changed. 'Not today,' he said darkly, 'today I am playing polo.'

> **Barbara Wilson, THE HOUSE OF MEMORIES**

When an American heiress wants to buy a man, she at once crosses the Atlantic.

Mary McCarthy, ON THE CONTRARY

Why is it no one ever sent me yet
   One perfect limousine, do you suppose?
Ah no, it's always just my luck to get
   One perfect rose.

Dorothy Parker, 'ONE PERFECT ROSE'

The hardest task in a girl's life is to prove to a man that his intentions are serious.

Helen Rowland

It is easier to keep half-a-dozen lovers guessing than to keep one lover after he has stopped guessing.

Ibid

Never trust a husband too far, nor a bachelor too near.

Ibid

So Jane considered her afternoon, didactically, a failure. But, in the smoking-room that night, young Cathcart explained the game all over again to a few choice spirits, and then remarked: 'Old Jane was superb! Fancy! Such a drive as that and doing number seven in *three* and not talking about it! I've jolly well made up my mind to send no more bouquets to Ton-Ton. Hang it, boys! You can't see yourself at champagne suppers with a dancing woman, when you've walked round the links, on a day like this, with the Honourable Jane. She drives like a rifle shot, and when she lofts, you'd think the ball was a swallow, and beat me three holes up and never mentioned it. By Jove, a fellow wants to have a clean bill when he shakes hands with her!'

Florence Barclay, THE ROSARY

Oh if thou lovest
And art a woman, hide thy love from him
Whom thou dost worship. Never let *him* know
How dear he is.

Letitia Elizabeth Landon, 'DESPONDENCY'

Her brother was not handsome: no, when they first saw him, he was absolutely plain, black and plain; but still he was the gentleman, with a pleasing address. The second meeting proved him not so very plain: he was plain, to be sure, but then he had so much countenance, and his teeth were so good, and he was so well made, that one soon forgot he was plain; and after a third interview, after dining in company with him at the Parsonage, he was no longer allowed to be called so by anybody. He was, in fact, the most agreeable young man the sisters had ever known, and they were equally delighted with him.

Jane Austen, MANSFIELD PARK

She had been brought up by a pious governess, of the sect of the Hernhuten, who thought much of female virtue. In those days a woman's being had one centre of gravity, and life was simpler to her on this account than it has been later on. She might poison her relations and cheat at cards with a high hand, and yet be an *honnête femme* as long as she tolerated no heresy in the sphere of her speciality. Ladies of her day might themselves fix the price of their hearts and minds and of their souls, should they choose to deal with the devil; but as to their bodies, those were the women's stock in trade, and the lowering of the sacred standard price for them was thought of as disloyal competition to the guild of the *honnêtes femmes,* and was a deadly sin. Indeed, the higher a young woman could drive up the price individually, the greater was her state of holiness, and it was far better that it should be said of her that for her sake many men had been made unhappy, than that she should have made many men happy.

Isak Dinesen, THE DELUGE AT NORDENEY

A bachelor never quite gets over the idea that he is a thing of beauty and a boy forever.

Helen Rowland

L'amour est l'histoire de la vie des femmes; c'est un épisode dans celle des hommes.*

**Madame de Staël** (d. 1817)

I cannot help thinking it is naïve of people who suppose they are in the upper strata of their organizations to complain because they do not enjoy their office parties. It is never intended that they should. That is not what office parties are for . . . An office party is not, as is sometimes supposed, the Managing Director's chance to kiss the tea-girl. It is the tea-girl's chance to kiss the Managing Director (however bizarre an ambition this may seem to anyone who has seen the Managing Director face on). Bringing down the mighty from their seats is an agreeable and necessary pastime, but no one supposes that the mighty, having struggled so hard to get seated, will enjoy the dethronement.

**Katharine Whitehorn,** ROUNDABOUT

The supreme happiness of the woman in love is to be recognized by the loved man as a part of himself; when he says 'we', she is associated and identified with him, she shares his prestige and reigns with him over the rest of the world; she never tires of repeating – even to excess – this delectable 'we'.

**Simone de Beauvoir,** THE SECOND SEX

How charming was, and is, the chanciness of being a girl. One has a kind of honey. But not for bees. You walk into a drawing-room and a dark man or a light man or a red man may change your life for no reason. The butler ought to whisper 'Cross my palm with silver' as you go in.

You might think that a woman of seventy-eight, glancing at a house where she was once in love, would be full of regrets. The extraordinary thing about age is that you don't regret love.

Even in the looking glass there's nothing to be done. The golden veil has blown off the face.

*Man's love is of man's life a thing apart,
'Tis woman's whole existence.

**Byron,** DON JUAN (published 1819)

It isn't that I was what's called, rather unhandsomely, 'highly sexed'. But it was such a surprise that one could attract. It was like a stream finding out that it could move a rock. The pleasure of one's effect on other people still exists in age – what's called making a hit. But the hit is much rarer and made of different stuff.

**Enid Bagnold,** AUTOBIOGRAPHY

There entered a young man who could only be Seth. Flora looked up with a cool smile.

'How do you do? Are you Seth? I'm your cousin, Flora Poste. I'm afraid you're too late for any tea . . . unless you would like to make some fresh for yourself.'

He came over to her with the lounging grace of a panther, and leaned against the mantelpiece. Flora saw at once that he was not the kind that could be fobbed off with offers of tea. She was for it.

'What's that you're making?' he asked. Flora knew that he hoped it was a pair of knickers. She composedly shook out the folds of the petticoat and replied that it was an afternoon tea-cloth.

'Ay . . . woman's nonsense,' said Seth, softly. (Flora wondered why he had seen fit to drop his voice by half an octave). 'Women are all alike – aye fussin' over their fal-lals and bedazin' a man's eyes, when all they really want is man's blood and his heart out of his body and his soul and his pride . . .'

'Really?' said Flora, looking in her work-box for her scissors.

'Ay.' His deep voice had jarring notes which were curiously blended into an animal harmony like the natural cries of stoat or teazel. 'That's all women want – a man's life. Then when they've got him bound up in their fal-lals and bedazin' ways and their softness, and he can't move because of the longin' for them as cries in his man's blood, do you know what they do then?'

'I'm afraid not,' said Flora. 'Would you mind passing me that reel of cotton on the mantelpiece, just by your ear? Thank you so much.' Seth passed it mechanically and continued:

'They eat him, same as a hen-spider eats a cock-spider. That's what women do – if a man lets 'em.'

'Indeed,' commented Flora.

'Ay – but I said "if" a man lets 'em. Now I – I don't let no women eat me – I eats them instead.'

Flora thought an appreciative silence was the best policy to pursue at this point . . .

'That shocks you, eh?' said Seth, misinterpreting her silence . . .

'I am afraid I wasn't listening to all of it,' she replied, 'but I am sure it was very interesting. You must tell me all about your work sometime. What do you do now, on the evenings when you aren't – er – eating people?'

**Stella Gibbons,** COLD COMFORT FARM

I loved the gentle girl,
    But oh, I heaved a sigh,
When first she told me she could see
    Out of only one eye.

**Lilian Curtis**

# A Ring on Her Finger

'Marriage is traditionally the destiny offered to woman by society,' wrote Simone de Beauvoir nearly thirty years ago. 'Most women are married, or have been, or plan to be, or suffer from not being.' This is still true today. Despite the number of couples preferring to live together in unwedded bliss, the large majority of women still feel that the Becher's Brook of life has been cleared when at last they get a ring on their finger. The uncertainty is over; they will be a Mrs rather than a near Miss. They can now cherish at least an illusion that their future is assured, and that they will have someone to look after them or to look after in life.

In this section Jane Austen describes how the betrothed state becomes a woman, while Helen Rowland, who often achieves an epigrammatic skill equal to Oscar Wilde, puts the male viewpoint. We have several proposals: pretty prosaic ones from Stevie Smith and from Mr Rochester, who deserved to have his craggy face slapped. Amanda Ros, who emerges as the Queen of Kitsch, shows Lord Gifford packing his beloved off home the moment he places the ring on her finger – perhaps to stop anything untoward occurring. On page 46 we have one of the most famous of Georgette Heyer's proposals, in which the beautiful Leonie finally arrests the rake's progress of her guardian, the Duke of Avon, in words that must have thrilled millions of schoolgirls, and grown-up girls for that matter. On page 47 Virginia Woolf brilliantly illustrates the haphazard train of thought which chugs a man towards committing himself.

Some pray to marry the man they love,
  My prayer will somewhat vary;
I humbly pray to Heaven above
  That I love the man I marry.

**Rose Pastor Stokes, 'MY PRAYER'**

An engaged woman is always more agreeable than a disengaged. She is satisfied with herself. Her cares are over, and she feels that she may exert all her powers of pleasing without suspicion. All is safe with a lady engaged; no harm can be done.

**Jane Austen, MANSFIELD PARK**

It isn't tying himself to one woman that a man dreads when he thinks of marrying; it's separating himself from all the others.

**Helen Rowland**

He told his life story to Mrs Courtly
Who was a widow. 'Let us get married shortly',
He said, 'I am no longer passionate,
But we can have some conversation before it is too late.'

**Stevie Smith,** 'AUTUMN'

'Leonie, you will do well to consider. You are not the first woman in my life.'

She smiled through her tears.

'Monseigneur, I would so much rather be the last woman than the first,' she said.

**Georgette Heyer,** THESE OLD SHADES

'Engaged?' she said. 'Well, I suppose that's very nice. Alfred what did you say? Who is he? What is that name?'

'He's a don, at Oxford.'

'Oh, dear, how extraordinary. You don't want to go and live at Oxford surely? I should think he had better go into politics and buy a place – I suppose he hasn't got one by the way? No, or he wouldn't be a don, not an English don at least. In Spain, of course, it's quite different – dons are somebody there, I believe.'

**Nancy Mitford,** LOVE IN A COLD CLIMATE

Should I marry a Foreigner? . . . You do not say, dear, if he is a man of colour. Even if it is only a faint tea rose – *don't*. I know what it will mean to you to GIVE HIM UP but funny things happen with colour, it often slips over, and sometimes darkens from year to year and it is so difficult to match up. *White* always looks well at weddings and will wash and wear and if you like to write to me again, enclosing stamped addressed envelope, I will give you the name of a special soap I always use it myself and do not stretch or wring but hang to dry in a cool oven.

**Stevie Smith,** NOVEL ON YELLOW PAPER

'Sit down beauty, I have something to give you,' said Lord Gifford, somewhat passionately. From his pocket he took a beautiful diamond ring and placed it on her finger. Then he said: 'Now, my own! my loved one! you can go home.'

**Amanda M. Ros,** DELINA DELANEY

As soon as our engagement appeared in *The Times* wedding presents poured in . . . the majority were frightful, and they came in cohorts -fifteen lamps of the same design, forty trays, a hundred and more huge glass vases. They were assembled at Grosvenor Place . . . When the presents were all arranged Lady Evelyn looked at them reflectively.

'The glass will be the easiest,' she said. 'It only needs a good kick.' She said silver was more of a problem. 'Walter and I had such luck, *all* ours was stolen while we were on honeymoon.'

Diana Mosley, A LIFE OF CONTRASTS

'You, poor and obscure, and small and plain as you are – I entreat you to accept me as a husband.'

Charlotte Brontë, JANE EYRE (Mr Rochester speaking)

No young man ever suggested anything to me but a wedding ring. They were emotional, violent in their protestations of love, and three men swore they would kill themselves if I wouldn't marry them. But I was untouched, adored, worshipped and wooed.

Barbara Cartland talking to the DAILY MAIL

He had been building one of those piles of thought, as ramshackle and fantastic as a Chinese pagoda, half from words let fall by gentlemen in gaiters, half from the litter in his own mind, about duck shooting and legal history, about the Roman occupation of Lincoln and the relations of country gentlemen with their wives, when, from all this disconnected rambling, there suddenly formed itself in his mind the idea that he would ask Mary to marry him.

Virginia Woolf, NIGHT AND DAY

I will uphold you, trunk and shoot and flowering sheaf
And I will hold you, root, and fruit and falling leaf.

E. J. Scovell, 'A BETROTHAL'

# The Deep Deep Peace of the Double Bed

Now to marriage, that remedy against sin, as the *Prayer Book* so charmingly puts it. Marina Warner points out in the first passage in this section that marriage as we know it today is a comparatively new custom. In the Middle Ages marriages were arranged by free and mutual consent. Not until the Council of Trent in 1563, several years after Henry VIII had rocked Christendom with his six marriages, was a church wedding deemed essential to validate the union.

The Catholic Church, in fact, had always emphasised the sanctity of marriage, and its motives for introducing such a ceremony were largely secular. In a society in which property is transmitted through the legitimate heirs of the father, it is vital to know exactly who the father is. The Church was determined to keep a tight control over the sexual activities of the male, limiting him to only one woman. This secular attitude underlies many of the moral attitudes of the Church, but from it has also sprung the concept of the importance of fidelity.

Women, being on the whole the more romantic sex, have higher expectations. If you've got to forsake all others, they reason, you must only marry someone with whom you are passionately in love. Even the most academic lady therefore has a terrible shock when she discovers that marriage, even to an adorable husband, doesn't extinguish desire for other men. The guilt she feels is splendidly illustrated on page 53 by Erica Jong. In a second passage on page 55 she points out that the very essence of romance is uncertainty, and having gained the security of marriage one then has to cope with the lack of excitement and incident – the rut-race in fact.

On pages 50-51 we see how great female minds over the years have thought alike, and displayed typical academic contempt for their own sex.

More contempt – indeed concentrated vitriol worthy of Swift – is shown by Martha Gellhorn, describing a revoltingly ugly couple on a train. Yet it seems unfair that the good-looking should have a monopoly of infatuation. Robert and Elizabeth Barrett Browning, according to contemporary reports, were both extremely plain, but theirs was one of the great love stories and each inspired in the other some of the finest love poems ever written. 'Browning,' wrote Francis Thompson, 'stooped and picked up a fair-coined soul that lay rusting in a pool of tears.' We have chosen one of her most famous sonnets: 'If thou must love me, let it be for love's sake only.' It is nice to think her request was granted, and she and Robert lived happily ever after.

Victorians had as idealised a concept of marriage as they had about children. It is interesting, therefore, to contrast the Elizabeth Barrett Browning sonnet with an equally touching poem on married love by a young American writer, Judith Viorst. Somehow, one cannot imagine Mrs Browning writing about scurf and acid indigestion.

In the twelfth century, the debate concerning marriage that had begun under the papacy of the great reformer Gregory VII (Hildebrand: 1073–86) became more acute. Was it the remedy of human weakness or a holy sacrament? The Church tried to prevent casual union and equally casual separation. Popes like Alexander III (1159–81) would have liked to enforce Church ceremony in the presence of a priest as the only contract to a valid marriage. But to do so would have rendered null and void (and therefore sinful) most contemporary unions. Alexander had to be content with the idea of free and mutual consent, sealed by sexual consummation. In 1215, at the Fourth Lateran Council, the Church tried to strengthen its hold by ordering the reading of banns and the public performance of the wedding, measures that would abolish, it was hoped, hasty marriages or elopements and make reversal or dissolution afterwards far more difficult. Benediction, however, was still unnecessary.

Given the Catholic Church's contemporary view on the sanctity of marriage, it comes as a surprise that matrimony was only definitively proclaimed a sacrament and the Church ceremony decreed an indispensable condition of validity as late as 1563 at the Council of Trent.

**Marina Warner,** ALONE OF ALL HER SEX

Her name was called Lady Helena Herring and her age was 25 and she mated well with the earl.

**Daisy Ashford,** THE YOUNG VISITERS

I know a lot of people didn't expect our relationship to last – but we've just celebrated our two months' anniversary.

**Britt Ekland**

It goes far toward reconciling me to being a woman when I reflect that I am thus in no danger of marrying one.

**Lady Mary Wortley Montagu**

I am glad I am not a man, for if I were I should be obliged to marry a woman.

Mme de Staël

The only reason I am glad that I am a woman is that I will not have to marry one.

Ida M. Tarbell on herself in Mary E. Tomkins'
IDA MINERVA TARBELL

Marion holds her bare white arms in the air.
'I'd never take me clothes off in front of a man.'
'But they say it's marvellous when yer naked.'
'Yeah, me mate what got married told me if yer take everything off, even yer bra, and yer get between the sheets and he takes all his things off too . . .'
'That's the thing about getting married, you can have it like that every night.'
'You just lie in bed, moonlight comin' in through the window . . .'
Marion shivers and climbs into the dress.
'If you love a boy and want to give him the best thing in the world there's only one thing, isn't there?'

Nell Dunn, 'SUNDAY MORNING' from UP THE
JUNCTION

In almost every marriage there is a selfish and an unselfish partner. A pattern is set up and soon becomes inflexible, of one person always making the demands and one person always giving way.

Iris Murdoch, A SEVERED HEAD

The new housing estate was on the outskirts of the town, it now took Trevor over an hour to travel to and fro. But the return journey was sweetened by the meat extract advertisements in the evening paper. These represented a young husband returning to a young wife, and though they changed slightly every month or so, their gist was always the same, the young husband commenting, playfully and appreciatively, on the delicious smell that the meat extract had given to a soup, a stew, or a plate of rissoles. During the years of living at home these advertisements had made rather wistful reading – not that he wished for better soups, stews or rissoles than those of his mother's cooking, but he would have liked to be praising Rachel for them. Now he could enter a home of his own, exactly like the young husband in the advertisement; and Rachel, turning off the Third Programme, would jump up and become the advertisement's young wife, and after supper and washing up would sit on the glacial arm of his easy-chair, looking forward to the day when they could have a television set, and being interested in the assorted womanly bits read aloud from the evening paper.

**Sylvia Townsend Warner,** A KITCHEN KNIFE

When you see what some girls marry, you realize how they must hate to work for a living.

**Helen Rowland**

The people people work with best
   Are sometimes very queer;
The people people own by birth
   Quite shock your first idea.
The people people have for friends
   Your common sense appal,
But the people people marry
   Are the queerest folk of all.

**Charlotte Gilman,** 'QUEER PEOPLE'

When a girl marries she exchanges the attention of many men for the inattention of one.

**Helen Rowland**

There was a famous Edwardian doctor who almost guaranteed an heir for £1000 – a fantastic sum, but worth it. Dr X was known to be almost infallible and many great families extolled his brilliance. He used, of course, an early form of artificial insemination. And it was whispered that the reason he never failed was that he himself was extremely healthy and strong!

Long after he was dead two of Britain's most noble and distinguished families were, in the 'twenties, united by marriage, but there was no heir. It was then remembered by those who knew them well that the bride and bridegroom were both the result of their parents consulting Dr X.

'Could it be possible they were brother and sister?' people asked.

**Barbara Cartland,** WE DANCED ALL NIGHT

Deborah was in despair. She had her code, she had summed up her life; marriage and all its cares, griefs and joys came into her sum of things. But passion was new, terrible. She had not realized the feelings involved in it. She had thought of herself as a wife, with the same emotions, the same poise, as she had in her maidenhood. To many women marriage is only this. It is merely a physical change impinging on their ordinary nature, leaving their mentality untouched, their self-possession intact. They are not burnt by even the red fire of physical passion – far less by the white fire of love. For this last Deborah was prepared; she had felt its touch without shrinking. But when Stephen kissed her in the wood, a new self awoke in her. She was horrified; she needed time to fuse the two fires, to realize that in unity they were both pure.

**Mary Webb,** THE GOLDEN ARROW*

And the crazy part of it was that even if you were clever, even if you spent your adolescence reading John Donne and Shaw, even if you studied history or zoology or physics and hoped to spend your life pursuing some difficult and challenging career – you still had a mind full of all the soupy longings that every high-school girl was awash in. It didn't matter, you see, whether you had an IQ of 170 or an IQ of 70, you were brainwashed all the same. Only the surface trappings were different. Only the talk was a little more sophisticated. Underneath it all, you longed to be annihilated by love . . . Nobody bothered to tell you what marriage was really about. You weren't even provided, like European girls, with a philosophy of cynicism and practicality. You expected not to desire any other men after marriage. And you expected your husband not to desire any other women. Then the desires came and you were thrown into a panic of self-hatred.

**Erica Jong,** FEAR OF FLYING

Marriage always demands the greatest understanding of the art of insincerity possible between two human beings.

**Vicki Baum,** AND LIFE GOES ON

---

*'Mary Webb died on 8 October, 1927. Obituary notices were brief and few, but Mr Baldwin pronounced an éloge on her work at the Royal Literary Fund dinner at which he presided on 25 April, 1928. Next day her name was famous. The lending libraries were beset by people demanding copies of her books, which were not easy to find as they had only been printed in small editions. In order to meet the demand Mary Webb's five novels were reprinted in 1928 with introductions by Stanley Baldwin, John Buchan, G. K. Chesterton, H. L. R. Sheppard and Robert Lynd' (DNB). Mary Webb's husband, Henry Webb, married again after her death; after his death, his widow, Kathleen, married Jonathan Cape, Mary Webb's publisher.

A husband is what is left of a lover after the nerve has been extracted.

Helen Rowland

Chains do not hold a marriage together. It is threads, hundreds of tiny threads which sew people together through the years. That is what makes a marriage last – more than passion or even sex!

Simone Signoret, DAILY MAIL, 4 JULY 1978

Family jokes, though rightly cursed by strangers, are the bonds that keep most families alive.

Stella Benson, PIPERS AND A DANCER

He'd nothing but his violin,
    I'd nothing but my song;
But we were wed when skies were blue,
    And summer days were long.
    . . .

But those who wait for gold or gear,
    For houses or for kine,
Till youth's sweet spring grows brown and sere,
    And love and beauty tine,
Will never know the joy of hearts
    That met without a fear.

Mary Kyle Dallas, 'BRAVE LOVE'

At the embassy we made the acquaintance of Harold Nicolson. 'You are very young,' he said to me. 'What you must do is to plant trees, *now*. Then you will enjoy them when you are middle-aged.'
'Yes, but where?' I said. 'We haven't got a country house.'
'Well, get one, *at once*,' said Mr Nicolson.

Diana Mosley, A LIFE OF CONTRASTS

But from then on he (the Earl of Berkeley) began giving me things. A house in California, a beautiful villa in Rome and other such gadgets.

**Molly Berkeley,** BEADED BUBBLES

I was not against marriage. I believed in it in fact. It was necessary to have one best friend in a hostile world, one person you'd be loyal to no matter what, one person who'd always be loyal to you. But what about all those other longings which after a while marriage did nothing much to appease? The restlessness, the hunger, the thump in the gut . . . the yearning for dry champagne and wet kisses, for the smell of paeonies in a penthouse on a June night, for the light at the end of the pier in Gatsby . . . Not those things really – because you knew that the very rich were duller than you and me – but what those things evoked. The sardonic, bittersweet vocabulary of Cole Porter love songs, the sad sentimental Rodgers and Hart lyrics, all the romantic nonsense you yearned for with half your heart and mocked bitterly with the other half.

**Erica Jong,** FEAR OF FLYING

I asked Shanti what the average parents' priorities are as they cast about for suitable mates for their young, and she replied without hesitation that all Coorgs consider 'blood' the most important qualification – by which I assume she meant caste and sub-caste. Next comes 'honour' (that is, moral character), and then property, health, looks and accomplishments. On the question of honour a boy's parents pay special attention to the character of a girl's mother and Shanti quoted a Coorg proverb – 'If the mother has a white tail the daughter will at least have a white spot'. So if a girl can produce a mother with an unblemished reputation it does not matter what unsavoury predilections she may have inherited from her father.

**Dervla Murphy,** ON A SHOESTRING TO COORG

Marriage must be a relation either of sympathy or of conquest.

**George Eliot,** ROMOLA

One man's folly is another man's wife.

**Helen Rowland**

Would you believe it? Lily asked herself. Would you think that a man and a woman, in their fifties, both so ugly that a solitary life in a cellar would seem their destiny, could go forth and marry each other, and display on their faces this look of embarrassed delight? The woman could hardly breathe for her chins and the heavy box of her breasts. She wore an electric-blue satin dress under her black coat, and her ankles rolled over the sides of her sensible black oxfords. The man was thin, with a neck that would not stay in place and supported his head loosely. His teeth were all out in front and long and yellow, and his hair either grew or was cut so that it started well up his head and sat on top like a parrot's crest.

They did not talk but, whenever they looked at each other, a secret and silent giggle shook them both; and the woman's face was purple with pleasure. Presently, seeing that the lady in one corner was reading, and the lady in the other corner turned towards the window, they reached for each other's hands, and two large swollen-jointed shapeless paws met and held. And both, with fierce discretion, looked at the floor as if they did not know they were holding hands at all.

**Martha Gellhorn,** WEEKEND AT GRIMSBY

We who have husbands at home should be very quiet, for we do not
know the meaning of days, nor yet do we understand the hush of
houses where in shadow go
   the unheard footsteps, the invisible faces of men.
Let us not speak
too loudly of war restrictions and rationing and black-out,
for there are eyes that seek
empty horizons, skies and deserts and sad grey seas,
and a sign from God,
while we who have husbands at home look in the shops
for wool, perhaps, or cod.
Let us remember when we complain of the winter's cold,
   there are others here
who have held in the moonless dark of a thousand nights
   the hand of fear,
and have walked for years in desolate barren valleys
   where no flowers grow.
We who have husbands at home should be very quiet
   for we do not know.

**Virginia Graham,** WE WHO HAVE HUSBANDS
AT HOME

Not all women give most of their waking thoughts to the problem of pleasing men. Some are married.

**Emma Lee**

In olden times sacrifices were made at the altar – a practice which is still continued.

**Helen Rowland**

Before marriage a man will lie awake all night thinking about something you said; after marriage he will fall asleep before you have finished saying it.

**Ibid**

Wedlock – the deep, deep peace of the double bed after the hurly-burly of the chaise-longue.

**Mrs Patrick Campbell**

It's not till sex has died out between a man and a woman that they can really love. And now I mean affection. Now I mean to be *fond of* (as one is fond of oneself) – to hope, to be disappointed, to live inside the other heart. When I look back on the pain of sex, the love like a wild fox so ready to bite, the antagonism that sits like a twin beside love, and contrast it with affection, so deeply unrepeatable, of two people who have lived a life together (and of whom one must die) it's the affection I find richer. It's that I would have again. Not all those doubtful rainbow colours. (But then she's old, one must say.)

**Enid Bagnold, AUTOBIOGRAPHY**

If thou must love me, let it be for nought
Except for love's sake only. Do not say
'I love her for her smile – her look – her way
Of speaking gently, – for a trick of thought
That falls in well with mine, and certes brought

A sense of pleasant ease on such a day'—
For these things in themselves, Beloved, may
Be changed, or change for thee,—and love, so wrought,
May be underwrought so. Neither love me for
Thine own dear pity's wiping my cheeks dry,—
A creature might forget to weep, who bore
Thy comfort long, and lose thy love thereby!
But love me for love's sake, that evermore
Thou mayst love on, through love's eternity.

### Elizabeth Barrett Browning, SONNETS FROM THE PORTUGUESE, XIV

It's true love because
I put on eyeliner and a concerto and make pungent
     observations about the great issues of the day
Even when there's no one here but him,
And because
I do not resent watching the Green Bay Packers
Even though I am philosophically opposed to football,
And because
When he is late for dinner and I know he must be
     either having an affair or lying dead in the
     middle of the street,
I always hope he's dead.

It's true love because
If he said quit drinking martinis but I kept drinking
     them and the next morning I couldn't get out of
     bed,
He wouldn't tell me he told me,
And because
He is willing to wear unironed undershorts
Out of respect for the fact that I am philosophically
     opposed to ironing,
And because
If his mother was drowning and I was drowning and
     he had to choose one of us to save,
He says he'd save me.

It's true love because
When he went to San Francisco on business while I
     had to stay home with the painters and
     exterminator and the baby who was getting the
     chicken pox,
He understood why I hated him,
And because
When I said that playing the stock market was
     juvenile and irresponsible and then the stock I
     wouldn't let him buy went up twenty-six points,
I understood why he hated me,
And because

Despite cigarette cough, tooth decay, acid indigestion,
    dandruff, and other features of married life that
    tend to dampen the fires of passion,
We still feel something
We can call
True love.

**Judith Viorst, 'TRUE LOVE'**

## Stay Up and Fight

For better for worse, for richer for poorer . . . the last section dealt with the 'for better' side of marriage, this one looks at the 'for worse'. The main battleground is shown to be between the different viewpoints of the man and the woman – between the husband who complains, 'I work myself to the bone supporting my wife and family. Why the hell can't she run my house properly?' and the wife who says, 'Just because he supports me it doesn't give him *carte blanche* to behave like a little Hitler.'

Nancy Mitford writes (on page 62) of a more privileged but perhaps more anxious age than our own, when, although a wife had servants to help her bring up the children, cook the meals and clean the house, she was neurotically dependent on the maids, cooks and nannies who carried out these tasks. If her husband complained about the pudding, the wife then had to reprove the cook in the kitchen, which might easily result in a fit of sulks or a threat of notice.

These bullying husbands also produced the ghastly martyred wives of Ella Higginson's poem on page 63. While any wife who's waited hour after hour, good will and beef shrivelling in the oven, for a husband to come home, a wait often punctuated by telephone calls from other husbands (because he's too much of a coward to ring up himself) absolutely promising he'll be on later and later trains, will appreciate extracts from Margaret Forster (page 65) and Katharine Whitehorn (page 66).

After such displays of male chauvinism, one cannot help giving three cheers when Mrs Penderton gives her husband his come-uppance. This passage on page 64 not only provides a telling blow against breadwinner power but shows Carson McCullers' writing at its most sensitive and voluptuous.

It is not true that life is one damn thing after another – it's one damn thing over and over.

**Edna St Vincent Millay**

There you are you see, quite simple, if you cannot have your dear husband for a comfort and a delight, for a breadwinner and a crosspatch, for a sofa, chair or a hot-water bottle, one can use him as a Cross to be borne.

**Stevie Smith**

The reason that husbands and wives do not understand each other is because they belong to different sexes.

**Dorothy Dix**

A man is *so* in the way in the house.

**Mrs Gaskell,** CRANFORD

It's really frightfully irritating, dear, how you take no notice of my rebukes or my comments. Upon my word, what I say to you seems to go in at one ear and out at the other, just like water on a duck's back.

**Ada Leverson,** LOVE AT SECOND SIGHT

Love-matches are made by people who are content, for a month of honey, to condemn themselves to a life of vinegar.

**The Countess of Blessington**

Alfred and I are happy, as happy as married people can be. We are in love, we are intellectually and physically suited in every possible way, we rejoice in each other's company, we have no money troubles and three delightful children. And yet when I consider my life, day by day, hour by hour, it seems to be composed of a series of pinpricks. Nannies, cooks, the endless drudgery of housekeeping, the nerve-racking noise and boring repetitive conversation of small children (boring in the sense that it bores into one's very brain), their absolute incapacity to amuse themselves, their sudden and terrifying illnesses, Alfred's not infrequent bouts of moodiness, his invariable complaints at meals about the pudding, the way he will always use my tooth-paste and will always squeeze the tube in the middle. These are the components of marriage, the wholemeal bread of life, rough, ordinary, but sustaining.

**Nancy Mitford,** THE PURSUIT OF LOVE

Forgive you? – Oh, of course, dear,
    A dozen times a week!
We women were created
    Forgiveness but to speak.
. . .

It's what you do, unthinking
    That makes the quick tear start;
The tear may be forgotten –
    But the hurt stays in the heart.

**Ella Higginson, 'WEARING OUT LOVE'**


The true male never yet walked
Who liked to listen when his mate talked.

**Anna Wickham, 'THE AFFINITY'**


I fear nothing so much as a man who is witty all day long.

**Mme de Sévigné**


Wretched woman that thou art
How thou piercest to my heart
With the misery and graft
And thy lack of houshold craft.

**Stevie Smith, 'WRETCHED WOMAN'**


One really rare possession she certainly had – a husband who, notwithstanding that he felt a mild dislike for her merely, bullied her and
interfered with her quite as much as if he were wildly in love.

**Ada Leverson, LOVE AT SECOND SIGHT**

I'm sorry to say my dear wife is a dreamer,
And as she dreams she gets paler and leaner.
'Then be off to your Dream, with his fly-away hat,
I'll stay with the girls who are happy and fat.'

Stevie Smith, 'BE OFF!'

Mrs Penderton's answer was a sudden laugh, a laugh both soft and savage, as though she had received some long expected piece of scandalous news or had thought of some sly joke. She pulled off her jersey, crushed it into a ball and threw it into a corner of the room. Then deliberately she unbuttoned her breeches and stepped out of them. In a moment she was standing naked by the hearth. Before the bright gold and orange light of the fire her body was magnificent. The shoulders were straight so that the collar-bone made a sharp pure line. Between her round breasts there were delicate blue veins. In a few years her body would be full-blown like a rose with loosened petals, but now the soft roundness was controlled and disciplined by sport. Although she stood quite still and placid, there was about her body a subtle quality of vibration, as though on touching her flesh one would feel the slow live coursing of the bright blood beneath. While the Captain looked at her with the stunned indignation of a man who has suffered a slap in the face, she walked serenely to the vestibule on her way to the stairs. The front door blew open and from the dark night outside a breeze blew in and lifted a loose strand of her bronze hair.

She was halfway up the steps before the Captain recovered from his shock. Then he ran trembling after her. 'I will kill you!' he said in a strangled voice. 'I will do it! I will do it!' He crouched with his hand to the banister and one foot on the second step of the stairway as though ready to spring up after her.

She turned slowly and looked down at him with unconcern for a moment before she spoke. 'Son, have you ever been collared and dragged out into the street and thrashed by a naked woman?'

Carson McCullers, REFLECTIONS IN A GOLDEN EYE

I went to a party the other night. At midnight, the host escorted a woman guest to her home. By five in the morning he had not returned. The hostess continued with her hostessly duties smiling politely. What else could she do? She is fifty, intelligent, and nice, but she is fifty. She

64

had been trained to behave well, and not to shout, scream or murder, and that is the only training she has had, besides cookery and housecraft at school. Her husband is rich; if it were not for him she would not be able to give a grand party, and in any case he will be home for breakfast which she will have the privilege of laying on the table before him. So what is she complaining about? What does she expect?

The woman guest needs comforting. Can one grudge her a simple sexual drunken pleasure? Her husband has just left for Norway on business with his secretary, who has long blonde hair and what her husband describes as laughing eyes. The secretary in her turn needs comforting because her boyfriend has become engaged to a plain fat girl who cooks Apfelstrudel and piles it high with whipped cream, and who came top in housecraft at school. 'A man needs two women,' maintains the boyfriend who is all of twenty-two, 'one to cook and one for bed. I love you but I shall marry her. As life goes on, sex grows less important and dinner more so.' The secretary, indignant as who would not be, zooms off to Norway in the woman guest's husband's Jaguar, for a month's straightforward affair with the boss, with a little shorthand thrown in. She prefers office work to cooking.

The hostess, fifty and at the end of the line of distress, smiles politely and offers hot soup to departing guests. Soon she will be a grandmother. That seems comforting, down among the women. One wishes marriage for one's daughters and, for one's descendants, better luck.

Fay Weldon, Down Among the Women


When Stanley came back she was still trembling with indignation. She burst out immediately, 'You've taken your time coming home, I must say.' Stanley took off his hat and gave her a long look that annoyed her to death. It wasn't what one could call a searching or penetrating look –Stanley was much too blank to apply such adjectives to. It was, on the contrary, a vacant look, if anything. It had proved very useful to him over a number of years, saved him from making a lot of silly mistakes. He had always employed this delaying device to great effect with his wife. Though at first it would produce anger in her, if he kept it up long enough it resulted in her telling him what all the fuss was about without him having to ask a lot of tiring questions and, if he could get away with sustaining his dramatic pause even further, she could be depended upon to solve the problem posed herself. Hopefully, Stanley held his hat in his hands and concentrated on The Look, taking care not to let the slightest glimmer of either amusement, boredom or bewilderment creep into his expression. He had only to move a muscle to bring disaster on his head. He had no wish for a late tea.

Margaret Forster, The Seduction of Mrs Pendlebury

'Being married means . . . how shall I put it? It means trembling lest Monsieur's cutlet should be overdone, his Vittel water not cold enough, his shirt badly starched, his stiff collar soft, or the bath too hot! It means playing the exhausting part of an intermediary buffer between Monsieur's ill humour, his avarice, his greed, his laziness . . .'

'You're forgetting lust, Renée,' interrupts Hamond gently.

'No, I jolly well am not! The part of mediator, I tell you, between Monsieur and the rest of humanity. You can't know, Hamond, you've been so little married! Marriage means . . . means: "Tie my tie for me! . . . Get rid of the maid! . . . Cut my toe nails! . . . Get up and make me some camomile! . . . Prepare me an emetic . . ." It means: "Give me my new suit, and pack my suitcase so that I can hurry to join her!" Steward, sick-nurse, children's nurse – enough, enough, enough!'

**Colette,** THE VAGABOND

Never go to bed mad. Stay up and fight.

**Phyllis Diller,** PHYLLIS DILLER'S HOUSEKEEPING HINTS

Well, time wounds all heels.

**Jane Ace**

My husband is a jolly good sort, one of those very hearty men. He wears plus-fours, smokes a long pipe, and talks about nothing but beer and Rugby football. My nerves won't stand much more of it.

**A wife at Tottenham Police Court,** DAILY MAIL

I have always held that it was a very good thing for a young girl to fall hopelessly in love with a married man so that, later on and in the opposite predicament, she could remember what an unassailable citadel a marriage can be, so, conversely, I think every engaged young woman should spend a lot of time in pubs as a preparation for marriage, saying: 'Ring her up and tell her you'll be late,' and seeing with what reluctance the commuters eventually leave; to go home to a spoiled dinner, a justifiably incensed wife and a feeling of grievance all round.

The old advice to a woman whose husband snored used to be 'Try sleeping in different towns.' This was regarded as a comic remark; but living in different places seems to be accepted as normal for thousands and thousands of couples. No doubt the country is healthier, cleaner, more natural, as rural pullets are better than battery birds; but free-range husbands would seem to me a high price to pay for free-range poultry.

Katharine Whitehorn, ROUNDABOUT

## The Battle Done

This section is about ladies who have loved and lost – sometimes lovers, sometimes husbands – and the strength of their loss seems to have inspired some of their finest poems. Many of these writers – Jane Austen, Emily Brontë, Christina Rossetti, Emily Dickinson – never married; perhaps their loss was intensified by the fear that they might never find anyone else to love.

The aim of true poetry, said Dryden, is to delight, and, one might add, to give comfort. Emily Brontë's haunting lines on page 71 are excellent medicine at times of emotional crisis and Alice Meynell's 'Renouncement' is almost as good as a stiff drink when one is waiting for the telephone call that never comes.

Jane Austen (page 72) claims that women love longer than men even when hope is dead and this seems to be the cry of the female condition. For, when a wife or a girlfriend pushes off, the man can straightaway ring up another woman and ask her out, but a woman has to wait biting her nails in the hope that one day a new man may turn up.

Some writers resort to satire when they are unhappy. There is a marvellously funny description of the rise and fall of a marriage by Augusta Gordon (page 71) and Judith Viorst brilliantly satirises the incompatibility that leads to the break-up of a marriage.

Death devours all lovely things;
   Lesbia with her sparrow
Shares the darkness, – presently
   Every bed is narrow.
. . .
After all, my erstwhile dear,
   My no longer cherished,
Need we say it was not love,
   Now that love is perished?

**Edna St Vincent Millay, 'Passer Mortuus Est'**

Ah tell me not that memory
   Sheds gladness o'er the past;
What is recalled by faded flowers
   Save that they did not last?
Were it not better to forget,
Than but remember and regret?

**Letitia Elizabeth Landon, 'Despondency'**

It is interesting to compare the above written before 1838, with the following, written in 1849:

Remember me when I am gone away,
   Gone far away into the silent land;
   When you can no more hold me by the hand,
Nor I half turn to go yet turning stay.
Remember me when no more day by day
    You tell me of our future that you'd planned:
    Only remember me; you understand
It will be late to counsel then or pray.
Yet if you should forget me for a while
    And afterwards remember, do not grieve:
    For if the darkness and corruption leave
    A vestige of the thoughts that once I had,
Better by far you should forget and smile
    Than that you should remember and be sad.

**Christina Rossetti, 'REMEMBER'** *

The sweeping up the heart
And putting love away
We shall not want to use again
Until eternity.

**Emily Dickinson**

I must not think of thee; and, tired yet strong,
   I shun the thought that lurks in all delight –
The thought of thee – and in the blue heaven's height,
   And in the sweetest passage of a song.
. . .

But when sleep comes to close each difficult day,
    When night gives pause to the long watch I keep,
    And all my bonds I needs must loose apart,
    Must doff my will as raiment laid away, –
With the first dream that comes with the first sleep
    I run, I run, I am gathered to thy heart.

**Alice Meynell, 'RENOUNCEMENT'**

---

*(Christina Rossetti's) *Goblin Market* is original in conception, style and structure, as imaginative as *The Ancient Mariner*, and comparable only to Shakespeare for the insight shown into unhuman and yet spiritual natures (!) . . . At the same time, though by no means immaculate, she greatly excels that very careless writer (Elizabeth Barrett Browning) in artistic writing and purity of diction. DNB

What a holler would ensue if people had to pay the minister as much to marry them as they have to pay a lawyer to get them a divorce.

Clare Trevor, quoted in NEW YORK JOURNAL
AMERICAN, 12 October 1960.

Sweet Love of youth, forgive if I forget thee,
While the World's tide is bearing me along:
Sterner desires and darker hopes beset me
Hopes which obscure, but cannot do thee wrong.

. . .

But when the days of golden dreams had perished
And even despair was powerless to destroy,
Then did I learn how existence could be cherished
Strengthened and fed without the aid of joy.

Emily Brontë, 'REMEMBRANCE'

Ah, once I loved thee, Atthis, long ago.
The fields about the farm are silent now,
Where in the windless evenings of the spring
We heard Menalcas singing at the plough.

Ah, once I loved thee, Atthis, long ago.
I shall not see thy face nor touch thy hands.
The empty house looks seaward: far away
The loud seas echo on the level sands.

Sappho, translated by Elizabeth Belloc

When we married we had a mews house and a poodle. I did my shopping in Knightsbridge and painted the house in sweet-pea colours, pink, blue and white. I had a baby boy with great difficulty and a lot of fuss. I later had another boy with even more difficulty, and we moved down to 'Executive Mock-Georgian House' in a Green-Belt suburb . . . Eventually 'Georgian House' became too small and Crispin began to think that Green Belt wasn't quite his image, and we moved to 'Stately Manor House' . . . Twelve years later Crispin walked out of our lives like a disinterested ghost and went to live in 'sin'. So far as I know he is being absolutely gorgeous with someone else. I wonder if he makes her sit at the chain end of the bath so that the chain makes a mark. I shan't be able to ask her as I shall never meet her, but if I do I shall say, loud and clear, for want of something better to say, 'Have you a chain mark on your behind?' And if she says she hasn't, I shall then know what was wrong with my marriage.

**Augusta Gordon,** Turn off the Peas, I'm Leaving

I know one husband and wife who, whatever the official reasons given to the court for the break up of their marriage, were really divorced because the husband believed that nobody ought to read while he was talking and the wife that nobody ought to talk while she was reading.

**Vera Brittain**

She always believed in the old adage, 'Leave them while you're looking good.'

**Anita Loos,** Gentlemen Prefer Blondes

All the privilege I claim for my own sex . . . is that of loving longest, when existence or when hope is gone.

**Jane Austen,** Persuasion

My life will be sour grapes and ashes without you.

**Daisy Ashford,** The Young Visiters

'Can it be that your attention has ever been, or is still, attracted by another, who, by some artifice or other, had the audacity to steal your desire for me and hide it beneath his pillaged pillow of poverty, there to conceal it until demanded with my ransom?

'Speak! Irene! Wife! Woman! Do not sit in silence and allow the blood that now boils in my veins to ooze through cavities of unrestrained passion and trickle down to drench me with its crimson hue.'

**Amanda M. Ros,** Irene Iddesleigh

Mark and June
Who were such a perfect match
That everyone used to say how perfect they were
Are getting a divorce, because
He only likes spy movies and Audrey Hepburn
        movies and movies that leave you feeling good
        and
She only likes early Chaplin movies and movies with
        subtitles and movies that leave you feeling rotten
        and
He thinks Maria Montessori is a fascist and
She thinks Will and Ariel Durant have an unwhole-
        some relationship and
He says she should pick up his socks and drop them
        in the hamper and
She says he should.

Mark is keeping the Honda
And June is keeping the Mercedes and the Picasso
        lithographs
As well as the Early American hutch table that they
        bought for a song in Philadelphia, because
He says it wouldn't have killed her to go on a
        camping trip sometimes and
She says it wouldn't have killed him to put on the
        velvet smoking jacket she gave him for Christmas
        sometimes and
He thinks Marshall McLuhan is a fascist and
She thinks Richard and Pat Nixon have an
        unwholesome relationship and
He only likes paintings when you know what it's a
        painting of and
She only likes paintings when you don't.

June gets custody of the children
And Mark gets their dog, their orthodontia bills,
And visitation rights on alternate weekends, because
He thinks a great meal is shrimp cocktail and filet
        mignon and
She thinks a great meal is something like brains
        cooked in a wine and
He says she is a fascist and
She says he and his mother have an unwholesome
        relationship and
He only likes women who'd rather make love than
        read Proust and
She only likes men who'd vice versa.

How come we thought they were such a perfect
        match?


**Judith Viorst,** 'THE DIVORCE'

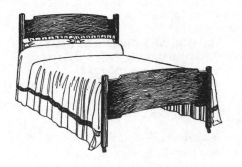

# Variety Is The Soul of Pleasure

Hugh McDiarmid said that the great discovery of the age was that women like it too. One suspects that this is rubbish and that millions of women over the centuries have been quietly enjoying themselves in bed, the only difference being that, except for a few pithy epigrams, they didn't talk about it much.

The extracts from Elizabeth Smart are remarkable for their lyricism. She wrote *By Grand Central Station* in 1945, long before the present vogue for permissiveness overwhelmed us. In the first extract we see the anguish of a woman whose lover is capable of falling in love with both sexes and this time has become besotted with a boy who has 'armpits like chalices'. This leads to the eternal question: Would you rather your husband ran off with a boy or a girl, or with someone pretty or someone ugly? The answer must be that it is always horrible. But perhaps, as Katharine Whitehorn once wrote of a woman and a man who were both going through hell sharing the affections of a comely but capricious wastrel, 'half a loafer is better than no bed'.

Women, in fantasy at least, seem to be drawn to men who give them a hard time (in the masochistic sense, anyway), which perhaps explains the fatal attraction of E. M. Hull's sheik when he first appears to the heroine (page 77). It seems sad, bearing in mind the huge influx of Arabian gentlemen into the more expensive parts of London, that they seem to lose most of their magnetic appeal when they leave the desert. No wonder they are happier as sandboys.

On the second night of his visit, our distinguished guest (Sir Charles Dilke) met Laura in the passage on her way to bed; he said to her: 'If you will kiss me, I will give you a signed photograph of myself.' To which she answered: 'It's awfully good of you, Sir Charles, but I would rather not, for what on earth should I do with the photograph?'

**Margot Asquith,** AUTOBIOGRAPHY

I don't mind the boys doing it, if they do it with their own class, but I won't have the girls doing it because they've got nothing to do it with.

**Rosa Lewis**

No man can understand why a woman should prefer a good reputation to a good time.

Helen Rowland

Accursed from their birth they be
Who seek to find monogamy,
Pursuing it from bed to bed –
I think they would be better dead.

Dorothy Parker, 'REUBEN'S CHILDREN'

I think all women like to dream about marvellous men. You know, real hero types. I've never met any of them myself, I doubt if anybody has . . .

I get my heroes so that they're lean and hard-muscled and mocking and sardonic and tough and tigerish and single, of course. Oh, and they've got to be rich and then I make it that they're only cynical and smooth on the surface. But underneath they're, well, you know sort of lost and lonely. In need of love but, when roused, capable of breath-taking passion and potency. Most of my heroes, well, all of them really, are like that. They frighten but fascinate . . .

Violet Winspear, in THE RADIO TIMES

Alas, I know he is the hermaphrodite whose love looks up through the appletree with a golden indeterminate face. While we drive along the road in the evening, talking as impersonally as a radio discussion, he tells me, 'A boy with green eyes and long lashes, whom I had never seen before, took me into the back of a printshop and made love to me, and for two weeks I went around remembering the numbers on bus conductors' hats.'

'One should love beings whatever their sex,' I reply, but withdraw into the dark with my obstreperous shape of shame, offended with my own flesh which cannot metamorphose into a printshop boy with armpits like chalices.

Elizabeth Smart, BY GRAND CENTRAL STATION
I SAT DOWN AND WEPT

Diana's eyes passed over him slowly till they rested on his brown, clean-shaven face, surmounted by crisp, close-cut brown hair. It was the handsomest and the cruellest face that she had ever seen. Her gaze was drawn instinctively to his. He was looking at her with fierce burning eyes that swept her until she felt that the boyish clothes that covered her slender limbs were stripped from her, leaving the beautiful white body bare under his passionate stare.

She shrank back, quivering, dragging the lapels of her riding jacket together over her breast with clutching hands, obeying an impulse that she hardly understood.

'Who are you?' she gasped hoarsely.

'I am the Sheik Ahmed Ben Hassan.'

**E. M. Hull,** The Sheik

My dear I'm never off duty except when I'm in bed – and not always then.

**Dorita Fairlie Bruce,** Dimsie Intervenes (the headmistress speaking)

I am over-run, jungled in my bed, I am infested with a menagerie of desires: my heart is eaten by a dove, a cat scrambles in the cave of my sex, hounds in my head obey a whipmaster who cries nothing but havoc as the hours test my endurance with an accumulation of tortures. Who, if I cried, would hear me among the angelic orders?

**Elizabeth Smart,** By Grand Central Station I Sat Down and Wept

A Bachelor of Arts is one who makes love to a lot of women and yet has the art to remain a bachelor.

**Helen Rowland**

A bachelor has to have inspiration for making love to a woman – a married man needs only an excuse.

**Ibid**

Of two evils choose the prettier.

> Carolyn Wells


Variety is the soul of pleasure.

> Aphra Behn, THE ROVER


'I am afraid,' replied Elinor, 'that the pleasantness of an employment does not always evince its propriety.'

> Jane Austen, SENSE AND SENSIBILITY


'She told me a good deal about Mr Driver,' said Jane. 'About his wife and other things.'

'Ah, the other things,' said Miss Doggett obscurely. 'Of course, we never saw anything of those. We knew that it went on, of course – in London, I believe.'

'Yes, it seems suitable that things like that should go on in London,' Jane agreed. 'It is in better taste somehow that a man should be unfaithful to his wife away from home. Not all of them have the opportunity, of course.'

'Poor Constance was left alone a great deal,' said Miss Doggett. 'In many ways, of course, Mr Driver is a very charming man. They say, though, that men only want one thing – that's the truth of the matter.' Miss Doggett again looked puzzled; it was as if she had heard that men only wanted one thing, but had forgotten for the moment what it was.

> Barbara Pym, JANE AND PRUDENCE


I am happy now that Charles calls on my bed chamber less frequently than of old. As it is I now endure but two calls a week and when I hear his steps outside my door I lie down on my bed, close my eyes, open my legs and think of England.

> Lady Hillingdon, JOURNAL, 1912

Love ceases to be a pleasure when it ceases to be a secret.

**Aphra Behn,** LOVER'S WATCH, FOUR O'CLOCK

In my first dream I was a Judge who was judging a young man who hadn't been very wise in his behaviour with a Boy Scout. This was my summing up:

'You are completely innocent and you leave this court without a stain on your character; *but don't do it again;* and I advise you in future to *employ girl guides.*'

**Christabel Aberconway,** A WISER WOMAN?

Every man has been brought up with the idea that decent women don't pop in and out of bed; he has always been told by his mother that 'nice girls don't.' He finds, of course, when he gets older that this may be untrue; but only in a certain section of society. The great majority of people in England and America are modest, decent and pure-minded and the amount of virgins in the world today is stupendous.

**Barbara Cartland,** quoted in SPEAKING FRANKLY by Wendy Leigh

She knew all the forms of vice to which the human flesh and mind were heir and to continue a career of evil she bought 'Modesty Manor', adopting the nom-de-guerre of Pear. Possessed of great personal attraction, her home was soon visited by all the Swanks of Seekdom within comfortable range of her rifling rooms of ruse and robbery, degradation and dodgery.

**Amanda M. Ros,** HELEN HUDDLESTON

When she raises her eyelids it's as if she were taking off all her clothes.

**Colette,** Claudine and Annie

Dined with Lady Willingdon (7 December, 1942). Emerald (Cunard) was 45 minutes late, as she so often and irritatingly is. At one point Emerald, with mischief in her old, over-made up eyes declared that no man was faithful to his wife for more than three years.

'That,' she added, 'is a biological fact.'

'You can never have known my Freeman,' Lady Willingdon retorted.

'Perhaps better than you think,' was Emerald's reply.

**Chips Channon's** Diaries

In the foyer he was efficient about checking them in, tipping hall porters, creating the right illusion of richness. She was efficient at looking away while he did so; both were connoisseurs of these kinds of expeditions. 'Isn't it nice the way the French take it for granted one isn't married and never ask for the girl's passport for the *fiches?*' she said, in their room . . .

'We should go to bed. Immediately. Or we will become embarrassed, and this expedition will fail. Which I don't want it to,' he said to Sarah.

'What extraordinary pants,' said Sarah, watching him undress.

'I know. I must get some new ones. These are a relic of my past. I once lived in Battersea and I came to the conclusion that the poor are differently constructed. I bought these there and they are the worst pants I have ever known . . .'

'I need some new pants too,' said Sarah, dreamily. 'Can we go shopping tomorrow and get me some? I'll only wear them when I'm with you, darling.' This gambit had got her a great many pants and other things in the past. It did not deceive Simon, but he said 'Yes'. After all, having committed himself to all this expenditure, he might as well get the best of it. And pants cost less than some things. But he was not looking forward to the moment when they would walk together down the Faubourg St Honoré. A happy thought occurred to him. Tomorrow was Sunday and the shops in the Rue St Honoré would be closed both on Sunday and Monday. This Sarah had forgotten. He realized this meant that he would have to keep her in bed for most of today.

**Venetia Murray,** The Twelve Days of Christmas

Platonic love is love from the neck up.

**Thyra Samter Winslow**


I am that twentieth century failure, a happy undersexed celibate.

**Denise Coffey,** quoted in the NEWS OF THE WORLD

# She's My Best Friend

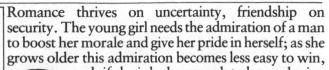

Romance thrives on uncertainty, friendship on security. The young girl needs the admiration of a man to boost her morale and give her pride in herself; as she grows older this admiration becomes less easy to win, and, if she is lucky enough to have a loving husband, less necessary, so she relies more and more on her friends for comfort and self-esteem.

'I like not only to be loved,' wrote George Eliot, 'but also to be told I am loved.' And both Emily Brontë and Jane Austen praise friendship as having more durable qualities than love.

A writer's attitude to friendship can be ambiguous, however. She tends to make friends easily because she is usually interesting, often witty, and because, ever on the look-out for material, she is an appreciative, uncensorious listener. She is less good, however, at sustaining friendships. Too much commitment to a friend gets in the way of her work and friends that suddenly drop in during the day and interrupt the train of thought are extremely unpopular, as both Countess von Arnim and Elizabeth Barrett Browning point out. Writers also tend to be indiscreet as a race, often selling the dearest friend down the river for the sake of a brilliant line of copy.

Possibly women writers' awareness of their limitations in the field of friendship makes them underestimate the capacity of women to be fond of one another. Gertrude Atherton and Germaine Greer (page 84) both comment on the superiority of men's friendships. This attitude always seems rather patronising. Just because two women are united by an interest in their children and their homes, why should their affection be any the less genuine than that of two men united by the racing results and fifteen pints each at the local?

One of Isak Dinesen's male characters remarks how sad it is that, although men and women can be lovers, they find it very difficult to be friends, perhaps because of the sexual tension between them. Only with a woman who is more a sort of chap can they really relax, as Elizabeth Jenkins shows on page 84. This quotation is taken from *The Tortoise and the Hare,* one of the most subtle and tragic of post-war novels.

Betty Macdonald on page 86 shows how upset women become if their friends don't conform to expected patterns, while Pamela Hansford Johnson shows how infuriating it is when an arch-enemy suddenly displays some totally unexpected virtue. We end with a poignant outcry from Judy Garland – a terrifying warning that even the most legendary superstars, whose names all are dropping and whose friendships everyone claims, can be lonely and friendless.

Why do we live? But to make sport for our neighbours and laugh at them in return.

Jane Austen, PRIDE AND PREJUDICE

I like not only to be loved, but also to be told that I am loved. I am not sure that you are of the same kind. But the realm of silence is large enough beyond the grave. This is the world of light and speech, and I shall take leave to tell you that you are very dear.

George Eliot, letter to Mrs Burne-Jones

The perfect friendship of two men is the deepest and highest sentiment of which the finite mind is capable; women miss the best of life.

Gertrude Atherton, THE CONQUEROR

We can say the brotherhood of man, and pretend that we include the sisterhood of women, but we know that we don't. Folklore has it that women only congregate to bitch an absent member of their group, and continue to do so because they are too well aware of the consequences if they stay away. It's meant to be a joke, but like jokes about mothers-in-law it is founded in bitter truth. Women don't nip down to the local; they don't invent, as men do, pretexts like coin-collecting or old schoolism or half-hearted sporting activities so that they can be together; on ladies' nights they watch frozen-faced while their men embrace and fool about, commenting to each other that they are all overgrown boys. Of the love of fellows they know nothing. They cannot love each other in this innocent, spontaneous way because they cannot love themselves. What we actually see, sitting at the tables by the wall, is a collection of masked menials, dressed up to avoid scrutiny in the trappings of the status symbol, aprons off, scent on, feigning leisure and relaxation where they feel only fatigue.

Germaine Greer, THE FEMALE EUNUCH

If you take a woman fishing, it has to be a dull one. Anybody lively scares away the fish. There's a special type of woman, in fact, who is chosen for fishing holidays. My uncle had a friend, old General

Mather, who used to take a particular woman away with him twice every year, simply to fish with.

And was she boring?

To madness, in ordinary life. But just the thing for fishing. And being in the open air all day made him very sleepy, so he needed someone dull to sit in hotel lounges in the evening.

**Elizabeth Jenkins,** THE TORTOISE AND THE HARE


A good neighbour, even in this,
Is fatal sometimes, – cuts your morning up
To mincemeat of the very smallest talk,
Then helps to sugar her bohea at night
With your reputation.

**E. B. Browning,** 'AURORA LEIGH'


This is such an out-of-the-way corner of the world that it requires quite unusual energy to get here at all, and I am thus delivered from casual callers; while, on the other hand, people I love, or people who love me, which is much the same thing, are not likely to be deterred from coming by the roundabout train journey and the long drive at the end. Not the least of my many blessings is that we have only one neighbour. If you have to have neighbours at all it is at least a mercy that there should be only one, for with people dropping in at all hours and wanting to talk to you, how are you to get on with your life, I should like to know, and read your books, and dream your dreams to your satisfaction. Besides, there is always the certainty that either you or the dropper-in will say something that would have been better left unsaid, and I have a holy horror of gossip and mischief-making. A woman's tongue is a deadly weapon and the most difficult thing in the world to keep in order, and things slip off it with a facility nothing short of appalling at the very moment when it ought to be most quiet. In such cases the only safe course is to talk steadily about cooks and children, and to pray that the visit may not be too prolonged, for if it is you are lost. Cooks I have found to be the best of all subjects – the most phlegmatic flush into life at the mere word, and the joys and sufferings connected with them are experiences common to us all.

**Countess von Arnim,** ELIZABETH AND HER GERMAN GARDEN


Friendship is the finest balm for the pangs of despised love.

**Jane Austen,** NORTHANGER ABBEY

'It is very sad,' he said thoughtfully, 'that you should think so little of us, for I am sure that all men that you have met have tried to please you. Will you not tell me why it should be so? For it has happened to me many times that a lady has told me that I was making her unhappy, and that she wishes that she and I were dead, at a time when I have tried hardest to make her happy. It is so many years now since Adam and Eve were first together in the garden, that it seems a great pity that we have not learned better how to please one another . . . For myself, I think that women, for some reason, will not let us know. They do not want an understanding. They want to mobilize for war. But I wish that once, in all the time of men and women, two ambassadors could meet in a friendly mind and come to understand each other.'

**Isak Dinesen,** THE ROADS ROUND PISA

A woman wants her friend to be perfect. She sets a pattern, usually a reasonable facsimile of herself, lays a friend out on this pattern and worries and prods at any little qualities which do not coincide with her own image.

**Betty MacDonald,** THE EGG AND I

The people I love are always somewhere else and not able to come to me, while I can at any time fill the house with visitors about whom I know little and care less. Perhaps, if I saw more of those absent ones, I would not love them so well – at least, that is what I think on wet days when the wind is howling round the house and all nature is overcome with grief; and it has actually happened once or twice when great friends have been staying with me that I have wished, when they left, I might not see them again for at least ten years. I suppose the fact is that no friendship can stand the breakfast test, and here, in the country, we invariably think it our duty to appear at breakfast. Civilization has done away with curl-papers, yet at that hour the soul of the *Hausfrau* is as tightly screwed up in them as was ever her grandmother's hair, and though my body comes down mechanically, having been trained that way by punctual parents, my soul never thinks of beginning to wake up for other people till lunch-time, and never does so completely till it has been taken out of doors and aired in the sunshine. Who can begin conventional amiability the first thing in the morning? It is the hour of savage instincts and natural tendencies; it is the triumph of the Disagreeable and the Cross. I am convinced that the Muses and the Graces never thought of having breakfast anywhere but in bed.

**Countess von Arnim,** ELIZABETH AND HER GERMAN GARDEN

Miss Blachford is agreeable enough. I do not want people to be very agreeable, as it saves me the trouble of liking them a great deal.

**Jane Austen,** to her sister

God gave us our relatives; thank God we can choose our friends.

**Ethel Watts Mumford**

You mustn't think I dislike little Lady Cunard. I'm always telling Queen Mary that she isn't half as bad as she's painted.

**Mrs Ronnie Greville**

Then if my friendships break and bend,
   There's little need to cry
The while I know that every foe
   Is faithful till I die.

**Dorothy Parker,** 'THE HEEL'

Mme de Saint-Loup called upon Mme de Cornnel and in the course of an hour observed, 'Madame, I was deceived in being told that you had lost your wits.'

   'You see', replied Mme de Cornnel, 'how impossible it is to believe what you hear. I was told that you had found yours.'

'She's my best friend. I hate her.'

**Richmal Crompton,** Just William

There are few things more disturbing than to find, in somebody we detest, a moral quality which seems to us demonstrably superior to anything we ourselves possess. It argues not merely an unfairness on the part of creation, but a lack of artistic judgement. We should be horrified to find, lurking behind one of Veronese's golden balustrades, a clown by Rouault, or an angel by Fra Angelico, no matter how gloriously painted either was in its own fashion. It would be both a moral and an aesthetic jar for us. We demand that people should be true to the pictures we have of them, no matter how repulsive those pictures may be: we prefer the true portrait (as we have conceived it), in all its homogeneity, to one with a detail added which refuses to fit in. Sainthood is acceptable only in saints.

**Pamela Hansford Johnson,** Night and Silence Who is Here?

If I'm such a legend, then why am I so lonely? If I'm such a legend, then why do I sit at home for hours staring at the damned telephone, hoping it's out of order, even calling the operator asking her if she's *sure* it's not out of order? Let me tell you, legends are all very well if you've got somebody around who loves you, some man who's not afraid to be in love with Judy Garland.

**Judy Garland** on herself, in John Gruen, Close Up

Oh, the comfort, the inexpressible comfort of feeling safe with a person, having neither to weigh thoughts nor measure words, but pouring them all right out, just as they are, chaff and grain together; certain that a faithful hand will take and sift them, keep what is worth keeping, and then with the breath of kindness throw the rest away.

**Dinah Maria Mulock,** A Life for a Life

Only solitary men know the full joys of friendship. Others have their family – but to a solitary and an exile his friends are everything.

**Willa Cather,** SHADOWS ON THE ROCK

# If The Devil Dress Her Not

Now to clothes – and one needs look no further than those covens of frumps at London literary parties to realise that women writers are seldom well dressed. Most of them are too pear-shaped from sitting at the typewriter or the desk all day to look good in clothes, and even the stylish ones like Edith Sitwell (page 93) seldom pay clothes the necessary attention to achieve true elegance. In spite of the best intentions, they usually end up with the kind of haphazard chaos described by Joyce Grenfell and Elaine Dundy.

Freya Stark, nevertheless, inveighs against the arrogance of women who dress badly, and one has only to look at the eager unpainted faces and baggy suits of most female dons, or to read Gertrude Stein's piece about Madame Picasso, to realise that many artists and most intellectuals have an arrogant contempt for anyone who takes clothes too seriously.

A suffragette once complained that before the First World War she had to wear an elastic band round her skirt while playing golf in case anyone saw anything. And after reading Consuelo Vanderbilt's splendidly graphic account (page 96) of the appalling restrictions of her youth, one appreciates what a liberating influence Isadora Duncan (page 95) had on female fashion. She must have struck as bitter a blow against the corset industry as Women's Lib ladies did against the bra trade in the seventies.

Men's reaction to women's clothes has always been a constant source of irritation. It's bad enough when a husband doesn't recognise a new dress unless it departs dramatically from the norm (Dorothy Parker, page 94) but even worse, as both Simone de Beauvoir (page 94) and Barbara Pym (page 93) point out, when he admires on another woman something he would disapprove of on his wife.

One occasion on which all women want to look both pure and beautiful is their wedding day, which is why Margaret Drabble's bride who got married in a grubby bra (page 93) made such an impression on all who read *A Summer Bird-Cage*.

A splendid remark came from Dame Rebecca West, who, at the age of eighty-five, picked a green kaftan off the rails of a shop in Sloane Street, and asked if she could try it on.

'But that's a maternity dress,' protested the shop girl.

'One can always hope for miracles,' said Dame Rebecca.

That nonchalant attempt of Eve's
To fashion garments out of leaves
Was not, as you have heard, inspired
By shame at being unattired.

**Mrs Harry St Clair Zogbaum**, 'AS IT WAS IN THE BEGINNING'

If it was the fashion to go naked, the face would be hardly observed.

**Lady Mary Wortley Montagu**


Boots and shoes are the greatest trouble of my life. Everything else one can turn and turn about, and make old look like new; but there's no coaxing boots and shoes to look better than they are.

**George Eliot,** Amos Barton


Englishwomen's shoes look as if they had been made by someone who had often heard shoes described but had never seen any.

**Margaret Halsey,** With Malice Towards Some


The magic of art is that it inspires inanimate objects with some of the qualities of life, so°that they can create pleasure, and satisfy obscure needs for colour, or rhythm, or form: the art of dress perhaps brings these qualities into the closest relationship with ourselves; and a woman who had no use for it must have some secret obliquity, arrogance or malady of soul. I suspect anyone self-satisfied enough to refuse lawful pleasure: we are not sufficiently rich in our separate resources to reject the graces of the universe when offered; it is bad manners, like refusing to eat when invited to dinner; and indeed I should call humility in religion the equivalent of good manners in ordinary life.

**Freya Stark,** Perseus in the Wind


Clothes? Oh, yes, I like clothes – on other people. Well, somehow they seem to suffer a sea-change when they get on to me. They look quite promising in the shop; and not entirely without hope when I get them back into my wardrobe. But then, when I put them on they tend to deteriorate with a very strange rapidity and one feels so sorry for them.

**Joyce Grenfell,** Stately as a Galleon


She found herself quite unable to look at Prudence, whose eyelids were startlingly and embarrassingly green, glistening with some greasy preparation which had little flecks of silver in it. Was this what one had to do nowadays when one was unmarried? she wondered. What hard work it must be, always remembering to add these little touches; there was something primitive about it, like the young African smearing himself with red cam-wood before he went courting. The odd and rather irritating thing about it was, though, that Nicholas was gazing at Prudence with admiration; it was quite noticeable. So it really did work. Jane studied her own face in the looking-glass above the sideboard and it looked to her just the same as when Nicholas used to gaze at it with admiration. Would he look at her with renewed interest if she had green eyelids? she wondered.

Barbara Pym, JANE AND PRUDENCE

She seemed to like my doing it for her, but I didn't like the physical closeness. I wasn't used to her. She was never a one for touching people, for kissing or fighting or sitting on knees. There were a lot of little buttons, all the way down from the demure high neck to the waist, and I fumbled over them. They didn't have proper buttonholes but horrid little fabric loops. I could feel her hard breasts rising and falling under my clumsy hand in her far from new brassiere. I thought how like her to wear a bra that is actually dirty on her wedding day. She must have been wearing it for the past week.

Margaret Drabble, A SUMMER BIRD-CAGE

My bridegroom's first words to me when I joined him at the altar were, 'Who are you?' It made me think that the hours I spent on myself before going to church were all worth while.

Letter in the DAILY MIRROR

The trouble with most Englishwomen is that they *will* dress as if they had been a mouse in a previous incarnation . . . they do not want to attract attention.

Edith Sitwell, HOW TO WEAR DRAMATIC CLOTHES

Why not be oneself? That is the whole secret of a successful appearance. If one is a greyhound, why try to look like a Pekingese?

Edith Sitwell, WHY I LOOK AS I DO

While some women, however, assert that they 'dress for themselves', we have seen that even in narcissism being observed by others is implied. Women fond of dress are hardly ever, except among the insane, entirely satisfied not to be seen. Usually they want witnesses.

**Simone de Beauvoir**, THE SECOND SEX

Nothing irritates a woman more than to see her husband admire in another woman the clothes and behaviour which he criticizes in her case. It should be said, moreover, that he is too close to her to see her; to him her face is always the same; he does not notice either her new toilette or her changes in hair-do. Even a loving husband or an ardent lover will often be indifferent to a woman's clothes. If they love her intensely in the nude, even the most becoming costumes do no more than conceal her; and she will be as dear to them when poorly dressed or tired out as when dazzling. If they no longer love her, the most flattering clothes will not do any good.

**Ibid**

She bought a new dress; black — he liked black dresses — simple — he liked plain dresses — and so expensive she would not think of its price...
'Do you really like my dress?'
'Oh, yes,' he said. 'I always liked that dress on you.'
It was as if she turned to wood. 'This dress,' she said, enunciating with insulting distinctness, 'is brand new. I have never had it on before in my life. In case you're interested, I bought it especially for this occasion.'
'I'm sorry, honey,' he said. 'Oh, sure, now I see it's not the other one at all. I think it's great. I like you in black.'
'At moments like this,' she said, 'I almost wish I were in it for another reason.'

**Dorothy Parker**, THE LOVELY LEAVE

If men were really what they profess to be they would not compel women to dress so that the facilities for vice would always be so easy.

**Mary Edwards Walker**

Glamour is what makes a man ask for your telephone number. But it also is what makes a woman ask for the name of your dressmaker.

**Lily Dache,** Woman's Home Companion, July 1955

The softer a man's head, the louder his socks.

**Helen Rowland**

Miss Ferber, who was fond of wearing tailored suits, showed up at the Round Table one afternoon sporting a new suit similar to one Noël Coward was wearing. 'You look almost like a man,' Coward said, as he greeted her. 'So', Miss Ferber replied, 'do you.'

**Robert E. Drennan,** Wit's End

It is difficult to see why lace should be so expensive; it is mostly holes.

**Mary Wilson Little**

Nothing is more debasing for a real man than a plastic apron.

**Lady Lewisham**

A Paris *couturier* once said woman's modern freedom in dress is largely due to Isadora (Duncan). She was the first artiste to appear uncinctured, barefooted, and free. She arrived like a glorious bounding Minerva in the midst of a cautious corseted decade. The clergy, hearing of (though supposedly without ever seeing) her bare calf, denounced it as violently as if it had been golden. Despite its longings, for a moment America hesitated, puritanism rather than poetry coupling lewd and nude in rhyme. But Isadora, originally from California but by then from Berlin, Paris and other points, arrived bearing her gifts as a Greek. She came like a figure from the Elgin marbles. The world over, and in America particularly, Greek sculpture was recognized to be almost notorious for its purity. The overpowering sentiment for Hellenic culture, even in the unschooled United States, silenced the outcries. Isadora had come as antique art and with such backing she became a cult.

**Janet Flanner,** Paris Was Yesterday

Brevity is the soul of lingerie.

Dorothy Parker

It is principally for the sake of the leg that a change in the dress of man is so much to be desired . . . The leg is the best part of the figure . . . and the best leg is the man's. Man should no longer disguise the long lines, the strong forms, in those lengths of piping or tubing that are of all garments the most stupid.

Alice Meynell, UNSTABLE EQUILIBRIUM

I have a theory about their (Englishwomen's) hats. I think they keep them suspended on pulleys from the bedroom ceiling and when they want to put one on, they go and stand directly under it, pull on a rope, and it drops down, smack, squarely on top of the head. Then, without touching a finger to it, they march out of the house.

Margaret Halsey, WITH MALICE TOWARD SOME

A diamond is the only kind of ice that keeps a girl warm.

Elizabeth Taylor (actress)

I got a wolf whistle in Covent Garden which reassured me (but I didn't need reassurance). What an effect one made in fine clothes when one was young! In those days the bus drivers would whistle when I wore a new hat. Not because I was beautiful, but because I was at last vain. I peacocked and a sort of sun shone out of me of self-delight.

Enid Bagnold, AUTOBIOGRAPHY

'What the hell are you doing in the middle of the morning with an *evening* dress on?' he asked me finally.

'Sorry about that,' I said quickly, 'but it's all I've got to wear. My laundry hasn't come back yet . . . I thought if I wore this red leather belt with it people wouldn't actually notice.'

**Elaine Dundy**, The Dud Avocado

As I was saying Fernande, who was then living with Picasso and had been living with him a long time that is to say they were all twenty-four years old at that time but they had been together a long time, Fernande was the first wife of a genius I sat with and she was not the least amusing. We talked hats. Fernande had two subjects hats and perfume. This first day we talked hats. She liked hats, she had the true french feeling about a hat, if a hat did not provoke some witticism from a man in the street the hat was not a success. Later on once in Montmartre she and I were walking together. She had on a large yellow hat and I had on a much smaller blue one. As we were walking along a workman stopped and called out, there go the sun and moon shining together. Ah, said Fernande to me with a radiant smile, you see our hats are a success.

**Gertrude Stein**, The Autobiography of Alice B. Toklas*

I'm tired of all this nonsense about beauty being only skin-deep. That's deep enough. What do you want – an adorable pancreas?

**Jean Kerr**, The Snake Has All The Lines

---

*Miss Toklas was incredibly ugly, uglier than almost anyone I had ever met. A thin, withered creature, she sat hunched in her chair, in her heavy tweed suit and her thick lisle stockings, impregnable and indifferent. She had a huge nose, a dark moustache, and her dark-dyed hair was combed into absurd bangs over her forehead.

Otto Friedrich, 'The Grave of Alice B. Toklas' in Esquire, January 1968

## Come Away, Poverty's Catching

This brief section deals with money and the lack of it – a subject about which women were traditionally supposed not to worry their pretty heads. Many of them, like the young Victorian wife (M. V. Hughes on page 101), were only too happy to leave everything to their husbands. But it was not so easy for single women, as Jane Austen points out, in the days when there was no old age pension and only a limited number of jobs considered respectable for gentlewomen. Aphra Behn and Colette come to the same conclusions on the contagiousness of poverty. People avoid you when you are in financial straits not merely because you might tap them for a loan and you can't provide hospitality any more, but also because it is impossible to be good company when you are beset with financial worries.

As a cousin of mine once said about money, money is always there but the pockets change, it is not in the same pockets after a change, and that is all there is to say about money.

**Gertrude Stein**


If this man had not twelve thousand a year, he would be a very stupid fellow.

**Jane Austen, MANSFIELD PARK**


During the late Irish rebellion there was a banker to whom they (the rebels) had a particular dislike . . . Accordingly they got possession of as many of his bank-notes as they could and made a bonfire of them.

**Maria Edgeworth, ESSAY ON IRISH BULLS**


In the midst of life we are in debt.

**Ethel Watts Mumford**


A fool and her money are soon counted.

**Helen Rowland**

Though only God can *make* a tree
Money can move them where they'll be.
A daily inspiration to
New Yorkers on Fifth Avenue.

> **Margaret Fishback, 'PUTTING FIFTH AVENUE IN THE SHADE'**

European society (society, that is, in its narrowest sense) automatically assumes its superiority to Americans whether they have money or not, but money tends to blur the sharpness of the distinction.

> **Virgilia Peterson, A MATTER OF LIFE AND DEATH**

The English have refined upon our naive American way of judging people by how much money they happen to have at the moment. The subtler English criterion is how much expensive upper-class education they have been able to afford. Consequently, in England, having had money (provided it was not too mushroomy a phase) is just as acceptable as having it, since the upper-class mannerisms persist even after the bank-roll has disappeared. But never having had money is unforgiveable and can only be atoned for by never trying to get any.

> **Margaret Halsey, WITH MALICE TOWARDS SOME**

A single woman with a narrow income must be a ridiculous old maid, the proper sport of boys and girls; but a single woman of good fortune is always respectable, and may be as sensible and pleasant as anybody else.

> **Jane Austen, EMMA**

Success to me is having ten honeydew melons and eating only the top half of each one.

> **Barbra Streisand, LIFE, 20 SEPTEMBER 1963**

Children love to sleep in houses other than their own and to eat at a neighbour's table; on such occasions they behave themselves decently and are proud. The people in the town were likewise proud when sitting at the tables in the café. They washed before coming to Miss Amelia's, and scraped their feet very politely on the threshold as they entered the café. There, for a few hours at least, the deep bitter knowing that you are not worth much in this world could be laid low.

> **Carson McCullers, THE BALLAD OF THE SAD CAFÉ**

Jane is rather like one of those refined persons who go out to sew for the rich because they cannot abide contact with the poor.

Colette, THE OTHER ONE


I never hated a man enough to give him his diamonds back.

Zsa Zsa Gabor


The tailor replied 'Simpkin – we shall make our fortune, but I am worn to a ravelling. Take this groat (which is our last fourpence) . . . and with the last penny of our fourpence buy me one penn'orth of cherry-coloured silk. But do not lose the last penny of the fourpence, Simpkin, or I am undone and worn to a thread-paper, for I have NO MORE TWIST.'

Beatrix Potter, THE TAILOR OF GLOUCESTER


Back from dinner, where I sat next to a young Canadian architect who lives and works in the next county. We got along well. I asked him, in comparing notes on English and American civilization, whether there is much graft in this country (England). He smiled. 'They don't call it graft,' he said. 'It's all done with so much Old World charm that it's quite painless. The Rape of the Sabine Women set to a minuet.'

Margaret Halsey, WITH MALICE TOWARDS SOME


One of the pleasantest things in married life is that you have no money of your own, but have to come to your husband for every sixpence. Here mother and I saw precisely eye to eye, for we both hated money calculations.

M. V. Hughes, A LONDON GIRL OF THE 1880s


Doorman – a genius who can open the door of your car with one hand, help you in with the other, and still have one left for the tip.

Dorothy Kilgallen


One must be poor to know the luxury of giving.

George Eliot, MIDDLEMARCH


Come away: poverty's catching.

Aphra Behn, THE ROVER

# Kissing Don't Last

'Kissing don't last, cookery do,' wrote George Meredith, and certainly few writers have done more to oil the matrimonial wheels of others, and to add to the sum of human happiness, than those great cookery writers Mrs Beeton and Elizabeth David. Mrs Beeton was as much sought after for her beauty as her cooking skills, and we start this section with her advising wives on the importance of producing delicious meals at home to keep their husbands from dining out every night. Mrs Beeton was a great cook; Elizabeth David is a great writer, combining practicality and simplicity with lyricism. On page 105 she makes one's mouth water describing the results of skilful marketing in a French household. During her first flush of popularity when the whole of the middle classes were trying out her recipes for daubes and *coq au vin,* a friend went to interview her and was invited to stay for dinner. He was totally enchanted by her lack of pretension. She matched him drink for drink for several hours, then, muttering that she'd better do something about dinner, went off and threw two partridges into the oven, and returned to match him for several more hours until the partridges were burnt to a cinder!

One of Mrs David's favourite source books (and presumably sauce books) and one that obviously influenced her literary style was *Les Bons Plats de France* by Mme Léon Daudet, from which we quote a sun-drenched account of Provençal cooking.

Anyone who reads the usual flat prose of cookery correspondents will appreciate how hard it is to write well about food. Virginia Woolf succeeds triumphantly in the two passages on pages 104 and 106. In the first, from *To the Lighthouse,* one can actually smell the olive oil and the wine, taste the bayleaves and the thick gravy, see the shining walls of the casserole, and the brown and yellow meats, so tender that one can almost hear the ring on the plate as the knife sinks through them.

Almost better is her description of lunch in college (Lord David Cecil believes it to be King's College, Cambridge), in which she captures that mellow euphoria and sense of rightness with the world that follows wonderful food, scintillating company and orbiting decanters.

It is interesting that, although she was one of the most voluptuous writers about food, Virginia Woolf suffered from acute anorexia nervosa. Likewise, the sexually inexperienced Emily Brontë wrote so powerfully about dark and unbridled passion. Perhaps, to misquote Emily Dickinson, excess is counted sweetest by those who ne'er exceed.

Slimming fads and practices were among the major bores of the seventies. On page 105-6 Fran Lebowitz, a New York journalist hailed as a latter-day Dorothy Parker, attacks stingy hostesses, raw carrots, and cold soup. Finally we have an even funnier American writer, Elaine Dundy. This extract from her novel, *The Dud Avocado,* shows cringe-making cousin John arriving in Paris and giving a waiter a very un-French dressing down.

I have always thought that there is a no more fruitful source of family discontent than badly cooked dinners and untidy ways. Men are now so well served out of doors at clubs, hotels and restaurants – that to compete with the attractions of these places, a mistress must be thoroughly acquainted with the theory and practice of cookery as well as all the other arts of making and keeping a comfortable home.

Isabella Beeton, HOUSEHOLD MANAGEMENT

Preserve a respectful demeanour
    When you are brought into the room;
Don't stare at the guests while they're eating,
    No matter how much they consume.

Carolyn Wells, TO A BAKED FISH

Do you know how helpless you feel if you have a full cup of coffee in your hand and you start to sneeze?

Jean Kerr, MARY, MARY

Years ago when a man began to notice that if he stood up on the subway he was immediately replaced by *two* people, he figured he was getting too fat.

Jean Kerr, PLEASE DON'T EAT THE DAISIES

An exquisite scent of olives and oil and juice rose from the great brown dish as Marthe, with a little flourish, took the cover off. The cook had spent three days over that dish. And she must take great care, Mrs Ramsay thought, diving into the soft mass, to choose a specially tender piece for William Bankes. And she peered into the dish, with its shiny walls and its confusion of savoury brown and yellow meats, and its bay leaves, and its wine, and thought: This will celebrate the occasion . . .

    'It is a triumph,' said Mr Bankes, laying his knife down for a moment. He had eaten attentively. It was rich, it was tender. It was perfectly cooked. How did she manage these things in the depths of the country? he asked her. She was a wonderful woman. All his love all his reverence had returned; and she knew it.

'It is a French recipe of my grandmother's,' said Mrs Ramsey, speaking with a ring of great pleasure in her voice.

**Virginia Woolf,** To The Lighthouse

I do not think that the Robertots spent, as the French are always said to do, a disproportionate amount of their income on food. What with the bargains from Les Halles, the wine arriving in casks from Bordeaux, and cream and butter from their Norman property, their food was lovely without being rich or grand. Above all, as I see it now, it was consistent, all of a piece, and this of course was due to Madame's careful buying. There was none of that jerky feeling you get when marketing is erratic or careless. So what emerges from those days is not the memory of elaborate sauces, of sensational puddings, but rather of beautifully prepared vegetables like *salsifis à la crème,* purées or sorrel, and *pommes mousseline.* Many egg dishes, and soups delicately coloured like summer dresses, coral, ivory or pale green, a salad of rice and tomatoes, another of cold beef, and especially, of course, Léontine's chocolate and apricot soufflées.

**Elizabeth David,** French Provincial Cooking

I know of nothing more appetizing on a very hot day than to sit down in the cool shade of a dining room with drawn Venetian blinds, at a little table laid with black olives, *saucisson* d'Arles, some fine tomatoes, a slice of water melon and a pyramid of little green figs baked in the sun. One will scarcely resist the pleasure of afterwards tasting the anchovy tart or the roast of lamb cooked on the spit, its skin perfectly browned, or the dish of tender little artichokes in oil . . . but should one wish, one could make one's meal almost exclusively of the hors d'oeuvres and the fruit. In this light air, in this fortunate countryside, there is no need to warm oneself with heavy meats or dishes of lentils.

**Madame Léon Daudet,** Les Bons Plats de France

Summer has an unfortunate effect upon hostesses who have been unduly influenced by the photography of Irving Penn and take the season as a cue to serve dinners of astonishingly meager proportions. These they call light, a quality which, while most assuredly welcome in comedies, cotton shirts and hearts, is not an appropriate touch at dinner.

**Fran Lebowitz,** Metropolitan Life

Cold soup is a very tricky thing and it is the rare hostess who can carry it off. More often than not the dinner guest is left with the impression that had he only come a little earlier he could have gotten it while it was still hot.

**Ibid**

Large, naked, raw carrots are acceptable as food only to those who live in hutches eagerly awaiting Easter.

**Ibid**

Anne was an immensely popular girl at Oxford, not especially pretty but with a bright smile which worked wonders of free feeding. I remember one young man telling her bitterly when she was in her third year:

'Anne, you are absolutely made of food. Food paid for by other people.'

Anne looked absolutely amazed, and temporarily even hurt, before philosophically helping herself to yet more asparagus out of season – we were at the Bear at Woodstock at the time. I certainly thought it the most bizarre remark; only subsequent reflection has told me how true it must have been.

**Antonia Fraser, MY OXFORD**

The lunch on this occasion began with soles, sunk in a deep dish, over which the college cook had spread a counterpane of the whitest cream, save that it was branded here and there with brown spots like the spots on the flanks of a doe. After that came the partridges, but if this suggests a couple of bald, brown birds on a plate you are mistaken. The partridges, many and various, came with all their retinue of sauces and salads, the sharp and the sweet, each in its order; their potatoes, thin as coins but not so hard; their sprouts, foliated as rose-buds but more succulent. And no sooner had the roast and its retinue been done with than the silent serving man, the Beadle himself perhaps in a milder manifestation, set before us, wreathed in napkins, a confection which rose all sugar from the waves. To call it pudding and so relate it to rice and tapioca would be an insult. Meanwhile the wine glasses had flushed yellow and flushed crimson; had been emptied; had been filled. And thus by degrees was lit halfway down the spine, which is the seat of the soul, not that hard little electric light which we call brilliance, as it pops in and out upon our lips, but the more profound, subtle and subterranean glow which is the rich yellow flame of rational intercourse. No need to hurry. No need to sparkle. No need to be anybody but oneself. We are all going to heaven and Vandyck is of the company – in other words, how good life seemed, how sweet its rewards, how trivial this grudge or that grievance, how admirable friendship and the society of one's kind, as, lighting a good cigarette, one sunk among the cushions in the window-seat.

**Virginia Woolf,** A ROOM OF ONE'S OWN

The prohibition law, written for weaklings and derelicts, has divided the nation, like Gaul, into three parts – wets, drys and hypocrites.

**Mrs Charles H. Sabin**

How odd it is that a little Scotch
Can raise Dutch courage to the highest notch.

**Louisa Carroll Thomas,** 'LEAGUE OF NATIONS'

At the fish, the wine reminded him of a funny thing that happened to him the other day at the hotel. It seems that, lunching with his wife, he'd suddenly decided to have a little bottle of vino. He meant, dammit, he'd been watching everyone, even the children, having wine with *their* meals every day, hadn't he? Well, sir, he ordered some, and Christ, as he'd be the first to admit, he didn't pretend to know one bottle from another over here, so he left it for the waiter to decide. But this waiter – wait'll you hear – this waiter turned out to be a real meatball. You know what happened? This – this *French* waiter mind you, began pouring the vino into John's glass first! How about that? Well, he'd stopped him of course. *Ladies* first, he'd pointed out, and in his limited French he'd chewed out that sad sack plenty – the poor guy had a face *yea* long when he was finished, he felt a little sorry for him, the way he just stood there you could see he didn't *know* any better – but if there was one thing John could not stand, dammit, it was impoliteness to women.

**Elaine Dundy,** THE DUD AVOCADO

# The More I Like Dogs ... and Other Animals

Many writers find it easier to communicate with animals than people. Writing is a lonely profession, and dogs and cats provide affection and companionship without constantly distracting the train of thought with chatter. As most writers run on flattery, the uncritical adoration of the dog is also particularly gratifying. Dorothy Parker, for example, surrounded herself with dogs, few of them house-trained. One likes her less, however, when one learns that on taking a dislike to one particular dog she decided to starve it to death by only giving it one small slice of tongue a day. On page 112 we have another example of sadism. This long passage from *Daniel Deronda* shows George Eliot's genius at character building. From the vicious way Grandcourt taunts the dog that loves him most, one can tell what a monstrous husband he will make. His loveless marriage to the beautiful, wilful Gwendolen, whose spirit he breaks, is one of the most terrible things in literature. By way of contrast to Grandcourt's poor Fetch, Gwen Raverat describes one of her own childhood dogs, Sancho, who had a gift for kidding people that he was permanently ill-treated.

Children and dogs, of course, have a natural affinity, as we find in Frances Cornford's charming poem on page 111. Nancy Mitford's Radlett children also took a highly anthropomorphic view of their pets. Every time Linda Radlett's labrador was banished to an outdoor kennel, she would moan that 'Even if I took him out for three hours a day, and chatted to him for another hour, that still leaves twenty hours for him all alone with nothing to do. Oh why can't dogs read?' On page 110 we see Linda stricken by the death of an earlier dog. 'Never give thy heart to man,' goes the proverb, 'he lives too long, or to a dog because he does not live long enough.' It is perhaps this brevity of canine life that has triggered off so many poems demanding a heaven for dogs where they can meet their masters again. We quote one (page 111) in which Victorian kitsch reaches an all-time high. Here perhaps is the origin of the word 'doggerel'.

After so much dog adulation, the anti-dog lobby, particularly those who live in towns, will be relieved to find one discordant note provided by Fran Lebowitz on page 113.

The man who works with animals does not love them any less because his affection is motivated by self-interest. Ruth Miller's Tembeni (page 115) is a devoted shepherd, whose sheep have come to have more reality than the family he is working so hard to support.

On page 116 we have a passage from Ouida describing a horse and rider jumping which is so extravagantly overlaid with erotic imagery that one is not sure whether it is the horse or Ouida herself who is coming over the jump. By contrast, the description of the shooting of a noble and beloved horse from *The Well of Loneliness* (page 117) is as moving as anything in *Black Beauty,* and shows the power of Radclyffe Hall as a writer. It is a shame that people write her off as merely the author of a Sapphic apologia.

From mercy killing we move to the wilful killing of a deer in the snow. This is Edna St Vincent Millay at her best, capturing the beauty, and dignity, and yet the ultimate vulnerability of all wild animals. For the same reason, we have quoted almost in its entirety Leah Bodine Drake's lovely poem about the kindly and legendary stork, which is slowly becoming extinct in Europe. It seems a fitting elegy for all species – the whales, the elephants, even the butterflies – in danger of extinction.

'It seems rather funny,' said Aunt Sadie, 'in a way. I'd no idea she was so particularly devoted to Patricia, had you, Fanny?'

'Nervous shock,' said Davey. 'I don't suppose she's ever had a death so near to her before.'

'Oh, yes she has,' said Jassy. 'Ranger.'

'Dogs aren't exactly the same as human beings, my dear Jassy.'

But to the Radletts they were exactly the same, except that to them dogs on the whole had more reality than people.

**Nancy Mitford,** Love in a Cold Climate

Did you ever know Yap?
  The best little dog
Who e'er sat on a lap
  Or barked at a frog.

His eyes were like beads,
  His tail like a mop,
And it waggled as if
  It never would stop.

His hair was like silk
  Of the glossiest sheen,
He always ate milk,
  And once the cold cream.

Off the nursery bureau –
  (That line is too long!)
It made him quite ill,
  So endeth my song.

For Yappy he died
  Just two months ago,
And we oughtn't to sing
  At a funeral, you know.

**Susan Coolidge,** from What Katy Did

Don't make the mistake of treating your dogs like humans, or they'll treat you like dogs.

**Martha Scott**

High up in the courts of Heaven today
   A little dog-angel waits;
With the other angels he will not play,
   But he sits alone at the gates.

**Norah Mary Holland, 'THE LITTLE DOG-ANGEL'**

I had a little dog and my dog was very small;
He licked me in the face, and he answered to my call;
Of all the treasures that were mine I loved him most of all.
. . .

His body covered thick with hair was very good to smell;
His little stomach underneath was pink as any shell;
And I loved him and honoured him more than words can tell.

**Frances Cornford, 'A CHILD'S DREAM'**

I'm a lean dog, a keen dog, a wild dog, and alone;
I'm a rough dog, a tough dog, hunting on my own;
I'm a bad dog, a mad dog, teasing silly sheep;
I love to sit and bay at the moon, to keep fat souls from sleep.

**Irene Rutherford McLeod, 'LONE DOG'**

Ginger and Pickles were the people who kept the shop. Ginger was a yellow tom-cat, and Pickles was a terrier. The rabbits were always a little bit afraid of Pickles. The shop was also patronised by mice – only the mice were rather afraid of Ginger. Ginger usually requested Pickles to serve them, because he said it made his mouth water. 'I cannot bear,' said he, 'to see them going out at the door carrying their little parcels.' 'I have the same feelings about rats,' replied Pickles, 'but it would never do to eat our own customers; they would leave us and go to Tabitha Twitchit's.' 'On the contrary, they would go nowhere,' replied Ginger gloomily.

**Beatrix Potter, THE TALE OF GINGER AND PICKLES**

. . . all at once there began to be other sounds up above – the rasping noise of a saw; and the noise of a little dog, scratching and yelping! The rats dropped the rolling pin, and listened attentively. 'We are discovered and interrupted Anna Maria; let us collect our property,– and other people's, – and depart at once.'

Beatrix Potter, THE TALE OF SAMUEL WHISKERS

The dogs – half-a-dozen of various kinds were moving lazily in and out, or taking attitudes of brief attention – gave a vacillating preference first to one gentleman, then to the other; being dogs in such good circumstances that they could play at hunger, and liked to be served with delicacies which they declined to put into their mouths; all except Fetch, the beautiful liver-coloured water-spaniel, which sat with its fore-paws firmly planted and its expressive brown face turned upward, watching Grandcourt with unshaken constancy. He held in his lap a tiny Maltese dog with a tiny silver collar and bell, and when he had a hand unused by cigar or coffee-cup, it rested on this small parcel of animal warmth. I fear that Fetch was jealous, and wounded that her master gave her no word or look; at last it seemed that she could bear this neglect no longer, and she gently put her large silky paw on her master's leg. Grandcourt looked at her with unchanged face for half a minute, and then took the trouble to lay down his cigar while he lifted the unimpassioned Fluff close to his chin and gave it caressing pets, all the while gravely watching Fetch, who, poor thing, whimpered interruptedly, as if trying to repress that sign of discontent, and at last rested her head beside the appealing paw, looking up with piteous beseeching. So, at least, a lover of dogs must have interpreted Fetch, and Grandcourt kept so many dogs that he was reputed to love them; at any rate, his impulse to act just in this way started from such an interpretation. But when the amusing anguish burst forth in a howling bark, Grandcourt pushed Fetch down without speaking, and, depositing Fluff carelessly on the table (where his black nose predominated over a salt-cellar), began to look to his cigar, and found, with some annoyance against Fetch as the cause, that the brute of a cigar required relighting. Fetch, having begun to wail, found, like others of her sex, that it was not easy to leave off; indeed, the second howl was a louder one and the third was like unto it.

'Turn out that brute, will you?' said Grandcourt to Lush, without raising his voice or looking at him – as if he counted on attention to the smallest sign.

And Lush immediately rose, lifted Fetch, though she was rather heavy and he was not fond of stooping, and carried her out, disposing of her in some way that took him a couple of minutes before he returned.

**George Eliot,** DANIEL DERONDA

He was a brown water-spaniel, rather like Dog Tray in *Struwwel Peter,* and with the same reproachful expression. He was obviously born to be a martyr, and it was hard on him that he had to manage to be one without the necessary ill-treatment: like making bricks without straw. But he did very well, for he had a wonderful power of putting other people in the wrong. He would sit there staring at you; brown and fat and smelly; slobbering, and sometimes giving a heavy sigh; and however long a walk you had taken him, he made you feel that it ought to have been longer; and however many biscuits he had had, he made you feel that he ought to have had more. Frances tells me that there was a legend in her family that Sancho was nearly always kept chained up; this was entirely untrue, but it just shows the force of his character that he was able to impose this idea on them from a distance. In other respects, he was a worthy, but boring dog, and appallingly faithful. We had at different times several more interesting dogs; but, just because I have a weak conscience, Sancho remains in my memory as the principal dog of my childhood.

Gwen Raverat, PERIOD PIECE


It's wonderful the dogs they're breeding now:
Small as a flea or large as a cow;
But my old lad Tim he'll never be bet
By any dog that ever he met.
'Come on,' says he, 'for I'm not kilt yet.'
. . .

I laugh when I hear thim make it plain
That dogs and men never meet again.
For all their talk, who'd listen to thim,
With the soul in the shining eyes of him?
Would God be wasting a dog like Tim?

Winifred M. Letts, 'TIM, AN IRISH TERRIER'


The more I see of men, the more I like dogs.

Mme de Staël


There has been erected in the stadium an exact replica of a fifteen-block section of Greenwich Village. Twenty contestants leave buildings on the perimeter of this area, each walking three dogs who have not been out of the house all day. The object of the game is to be the first to get to the sidewalk directly in front of my building.

Fran Lebowitz, METROPOLITAN LIFE

I got a coat lined with hamster. You couldn't do that kind of thing in America. All the Boy Scouts would go on strike.

Suzy Parker, NEWSWEEK, February 1963

O lively, O most charming pug,
Thy graceful air, and heavenly mug;
The beauties of his mind do shine,
And every bit is shaped and fine.
Your teeth are whiter than the snow,
You're a great buck, you're a great beau;
Your eyes are of so nice a shape,
More like a Christian's than an ape;
Your cheeck is like the rose's blume,
Your hair is like the raven's plume,
His nose's cast is of the Roman,
He is a very pretty woman.
I could not get a rhyme for Roman,
So was obliged to call him woman.

Marjorie Fleming (aged 8), 'SONNET TO A MONKEY'

It was a little captive cat
    Upon a crowded train
His mistress takes him from his box
    To ease his fretful pain.

She holds him tight upon her knee
    The graceful animal
And all the people look at him
    He is so beautiful.

But oh he pricks and oh he prods
    And turns upon her knee
Then lifteth up his innocent voice
    In plaintive melody.

He lifteth up his innocent voice
    He lifteth up, he singeth
And to each human countenance
    A smile of grace he bringeth.

He lifteth up his innocent paw
    Upon her breast he clingeth
And everybody cries, Behold
    The cat, the cat that singeth.

Stevie Smith, 'THE SINGING CAT'

You did not sing to Shelley such a song
As Shelley sang to you.

**Sarah Piatt**, 'A Word with a Skylark'

They say the storks are leaving Europe, growing rare.
Those long-shanked gentlemen-fishers, farmers' friends,
Are leaving the Dutch swangs and the Baltic mosses.
There are empty nests upon the stepped Dutch gables,
The Jutland thatch, the sloping Flemish roofs
And high, windy wheels poled above German cabbages.

More ancient than the phoenix, he is painted
On neolithic caves, already aristocratic
Yet neighbourly, soon to step into fairytale
And to take under his wing men's newborn soul.
Faithful and tender mate, provident sire –
The Arabs wrote, 'Who kills a stork is an Unbeliever.'

Most merciful bird, he spiralled the Gallows Tree
Crying 'Be strong! Be strong!' to the Crucified;
And having heartened Love's heart with these few words
Never spoke again; but his big clumsy beak
Can clash a courteous greeting to his Lady:
They tell this beside the tiled stoves of Sweden.

But soon blond children will lift little cold faces
To gusty Gothic skies, hoping for, not seeing
Clatterwings, their kind fairy, their roof-angel,
Flapping up from Tunis bringing good luck and tulips,
To brood again on the brick stack, the ruined tower.
(Where does he go? To castles west of the moon?)

And Freiburg under the Schwarzwald, whose pines
Pad darkly down the slopes like a sloth of bears,
Will ring her great bells over the Munsterplatz –
Maria, Konrad, Michael, mighty Christ –
Calling the birds home to the steep ridge-poles
And see no storks in their lordly sunset musters.

**Leah Bodine Drake**, 'The Storks'

So, it was night. The cockerels were sleep-perched,
Silent, their king's heads thrust in feathered capes.
And the sheep were my friends. They knew me. Had I not
Fed them and led them, scanned the sky for storms,
Chased their ungainly gawky mass to shelter
When green was in the sky and I smelled hail;

Led them to scooped-out valleys, when the wind
Tore at their silly faces, the white snouts
Raised in a panic, grey milk in their eyes.
Taken their tottering lambs on steepled legs,
And fed them from a teat in a windy barn?
Most of my life was theirs, sheep-ministered, the while
My wife, my children, lay within their hut
Alone and fireless, and heard the hail
Tearing the silver tassels from the stalks,
And dreamed, or wept, or shouted with shrill shrew
Of pallid anger that would die in tears.

**Ruth Miller,** '**TEMBENI**'

White sky, over the hemlocks bowed with snow.
Saw you not at the beginning of evening the antlered buck
    and his doe
Standing in the apple-orchard? I saw them. I saw them
    suddenly go,
Tails up, with long leaps lovely and slow,
Over the stone-wall into the woods of hemlocks bowed with snow.

Now lies he here, his wild blood scalding the snow.

How strange a thing is death, bringing to his knees, bringing
    to his antlers
The buck in the snow
How strange a thing, – a mile away by now it may be,
Under the heavy hemlocks that as the moments pass
Shift their loads a little, letting fall a feather of snow –
Life, looking out attentive from the eyes of the doe.

**Edna St Vincent Millay,** THE BUCK IN THE SNOW

A cat that lives with a good family is used to being talked to all the time.

**Lettice Cooper,** PARKIN

Cecil's hands clinched unconsciously on the bridle, and his face was very pale – pale with excitation – as his foot where the stirrup was broken crushed closer and harder against the Gray's flanks.

    'Oh, my darling, my beauty – *now!*'

    One touch of the spur – the first – and Forest King rose at the leap, all the life and power there were in him gathered for one superhuman and crowning effort; a flash of time, not half a second in duration, and he was lifted in the air higher, and higher, and higher in the cold, fresh, wild winter wind; stakes and rails, and thorn and water lay beneath him black and gaunt and shapeless, yawning like a grave; one bound, even in mid-air, one last convulsive impulse of the gathered limbs, and Forest King was over!

**Ouida,** UNDER TWO FLAGS

They took Raferty in an ambulance from Great Malvern in order to spare him the jar of the roads. That night he slept in his own spacious loose-box, and the faithful Jim would not leave him that night; he sat up and watched while Raferty slept in so deep a bed of yellow-gold straw that it all but reached to his knees when standing. A last inarticulate tribute to the most gallant horse, the most courteous horse that ever stepped out of stable.

But when the sun came up over Bredon, flooding the breadth of the Severn Valley, touching the slopes of the Malvern Hills that stand opposite Bredon across the valley, gilding the old red bricks of Morton and the weather-vane on its quiet stables, Stephen went into her father's study and she loaded his heavy revolver.

Then they led Raferty out and into the morning; they led him with care to the big north paddock and stood him beside the mighty hedge that had set the seal on his youthful valour. Very still he stood with the sun on his flanks, the groom, Jim, holding the bridle.

Stephen said: 'I'm going to send you away, a long way away, and I've never left you except for a little while since you came when I was a child and you were quite young – but I'm going to send you a long way away because of your pain. Raferty, this is death; and beyond, they say, there's no more suffering.' She paused, then spoke in a voice so low that the groom could not hear her: 'Forgive me, Raferty.'

And Raferty stood there looking at Stephen, and his eyes were so soft as an Irish morning, yet as brave as the eyes that looked into his. Then it seemed to Stephen that he had spoken, that Raferty had said: 'Since to me you are God, what have I to forgive you, Stephen?'

She took a step forward and pressed the revolver high up against Raferty's smooth, grey forehead. She fired, and he dropped to the ground like a stone, lying perfectly still by the mighty hedge that had set the seal on his youthful valour.

**Radclyffe Hall,** THE WELL OF LONELINESS

## U-Phony

Women have often been accused of being worse snobs than men. H. G. Wells in 1905 went so far as to claim that 'there was no social difference till women came in,' perhaps because in those days they had more leisure in which to worry about the nuances of class. One has only to read the Women's Institute report with which this section begins to realise how class barriers have been broken down in the last seventy years.

Certainly Daisy Ashford could only have acquired such perfect social pitch by listening to the adults around her. On page 120 we see her hero, the *nouveau riche* Mr Salteena, accepting the fact that he is not quite a gentleman. This, however, does not prevent him from setting his foot on the social ladder with unashamed enthusiasm. One is more surprised to find the same emotion expressed by Charlotte Brontë. Margaret Halsey crops up once again to indulge in some Brit-bashing: the English upper classes have perfect manners, she says, they never insult the Mr Salteenas of this world, they merely don't ask them to dinner. Claire Sheridan explains how the training for this eternal politeness was carried out, while Mrs Alsop gives us a glimpse of Lady Sackville searching the ladies' lavatories of the British Embassy in Washington for lonely wallflowers, a practice one feels her daughter may have followed with less disinterested motives!

Ladies were certainly different in those days. They were so sure of themselves and had such an air of authority that they could get anyone to do anything, as Gwen Raverat points out on page 121. In their charitable role, they waged a perpetual war against sin, particularly when practised by the lower classes (page 122), without themselves having any clear idea what sin was. Their amazing self-confidence is further illustrated by F. M. Mayor (page 120); ladies were educated, but they never engaged in intellectual arguments because they knew they were right. Not for them the hours of introspection and self-doubt indulged in by women of the later twentieth century. On the other hand they thought it was immoral to waste all the leisure hours at their disposal on anything so frivolous as playing bridge. Bridge obviates the need for conversation, and therefore for any kind of effort.

Also included in this section is another splendid story about Gertrude Stein, this time suffering from hiccups. Perhaps it was during such an attack that Miss Stein first said: 'A rose is – hic – a rose is – hic – a rose.'

When the Women's Institute started at the turn of the century they were determined to cross class barriers. One president reported with satisfaction: 'We have done very well: we have elected five ladies, five women and one school teacher.'

Quoted in JAM & JERUSALEM by Simon Goodenough

I am fond of digging in the garden and I am parshial to ladies if they are nice I suppose it is my nature. I am not quite a gentleman but you would hardly notice it but can't be helped anyhow.

Daisy Ashford, THE YOUNG VISITERS

Towards people with whom they disagree the English Gentry, or at any rate that small cross-section of them which I have seen, are tranquilly good-natured. It is not *comme il faut* to establish the supremacy of an idea by smashing in the faces of all the people who try to contradict it. The English never smash in a face. They merely refrain from asking it to dinner.

Margaret Halsey, WITH MALICE TOWARD SOME

He is every other inch a gentleman.

Rebecca West

The good manners of educated Englishmen . . . are the most exquisitely modulated attentions I have ever received. Such leaping to feet, such opening of doors, such lightning flourishes with matches and cigarettes – it's all so heroic, I never quite get over the feeling that someone has just said, 'To the lifeboats!'

Margaret Halsey, WITH MALICE TOWARD SOME

The argument about bridge meant more than met the ear. There in a nutshell lay an important difference between the nineteenth and twentieth centuries – what is passing away and what is taking its place. If Kathy had probed her, Mrs Herbert would only have repeated it was a pity. The ladies of her generation were incapable of discussion. They were as inarticulate as the uneducated, though often almost erudite. And why should they discuss, since everything they thought was right? Besides, they never liked to expose their inner thoughts. Here Mrs Herbert's inner thought was *noblesse oblige*. It was wrong to use hours of leisure – she never questioned her right to them – on anything so frivolous as bridge. To play it scientifically would be the misuse of a talent. To that proud idea the upper middle-class owed its thousands of cultivated homes, now all crumbling away.

F. M. Mayor, THE RECTOR'S DAUGHTER

I like high life. I like its manners, its splendours, the beings which move in its enchanted sphere. I like to consider the habits of those beings, their way of thinking, speaking, acting. Let fools talk about the artificial, voluptuous, idle existence spun out by Dukes, Lords, Ladies, Knights and Esquires of high degree. Such cant is not for me. I despise it.

**Charlotte Brontë,** HIGH LIFE IN VERDOPOLIS

'B.M.' (Lady Sackville) fascinated me, for many of her qualities were opposed by a wholly contradictory set of qualities. At one moment she was a great lady, mistress of Knole and a friend of kings; a few moments later a peasant, giving one morsels of food in her fingers from her plate and saying, 'Eat this, eat this, it is so good'. Though in many ways she was madly extravagant, in others she was eccentrically mean. Either she wrote a letter on the most expensive parchment crested and monogrammed paper, or on lavatory paper. I think it was her daughter Vita, 'my little Vita,' who received a letter from her mother, written in the Ladies' room at Harrods, ending *'Voyez comme ce papier prend l'encre mieux que le bromo'.*

**Christabel Aberconway,** A WISER WOMAN?

Ladies were ladies in those days; they did not do things themselves, they told other people what to do and how to do it. My mother would have told anybody how to do anything: the cook how to skin a rabbit, or the groom how to harness a horse; though of course she had never done, or even observed, these operations herself. She would cheerfully have told an engine-driver how to drive his engine, and he would have taken it quite naturally, and have answered: 'Yes, ma'am,' 'Very good, ma'am,' 'Quite right, ma'am,' and then would have gone on driving his engine exactly as before, with hardly even an inward grin at the vagaries of the upper classes; while my mother would certainly have thought his driving much improved. But then they would both have been experts at their own jobs and tolerant of each others' little whims.

**Gwen Raverat,** PERIOD PIECE

She did not like her name. It was a mean, small name, with a kind of facetious twist, she thought, about its end like the upward curve of a pugdog's tail. There it was, however. There was no doing anything with it. Wilkins she was and Wilkins she would remain; and though her husband encouraged her to give it on all occasions as Mrs Mellersh-Wilkins she only did that when he was within earshot, for she thought Mellersh made Wilkins worse, emphasizing it in the way Chatsworth on the gate-posts of a villa emphasizes the villa.

**Countess von Arnim,** THE ENCHANTED APRIL

'I am not really a London person,' said Sir Leicester, reproachfully. 'I work in London, but my home is in Surrey.'

'I count that,' Aunt Sadie said, gently but firmly, 'as the same.'

**Nancy Mitford,** THE PURSUIT OF LOVE

He had not an ounce of spare flesh on his bones, and leanness goes a great way towards gentility.

**Mrs Gaskell,** WIVES AND DAUGHTERS

A lady, that is an enlightened, cultivated, liberal lady – the only kind to be in a time of increasing classlessness – could espouse any cause; wayward girls, social diseases, unmarried mothers, and/or birth control with impunity. But never by so much as the shadow of a look should she acknowledge her own experience with the Facts of Life.

**Virgilia Peterson,** A MATTER OF LIFE AND DEATH

She answered by return of post
The invitation of her host.
She caught the train she said she would,
And changed at junctions as she should.
She brought a light and smallish box
And keys belonging to the locks.

**Rose Henniker Heaton,** THE PERFECT GUEST

Human nature is so well disposed towards those in interesting situations that a young person who either marries or dies is sure to be well spoken of.

**Jane Austen**

Gossip is the sort of smoke that comes from the dirty tobacco-pipes of those who diffuse it; it proves nothing but the bad taste of the smoker.

**George Eliot,** DANIEL DERONDA

The two men paused in their conversation to watch Victoria and the visitor noticed how gracefully she danced; but that while doing so she kept a sharp look-out for new arrivals. At the sight of one she would break away from her partner, bound to the doorway and cordially greet the new arrivals, introduce partners to girls and attend to everyone. She led the way from the ballroom to the dining-room, saw that everyone was seated, and even looked into the dressing-room for ladies to see if all was right there.

Any woman reader who has ever been shy will instantly pick up the most important point in this description – Victoria's swift check of the ladies' cloakroom. She was not concerned about clean towels; an efficient maid would have been on duty. She was concerned about the lonely girls who at balls seek the ladies' cloakroom as a safe haven, pretending to arrange their hair.

**Susan Mary Alsop,** LADY SACKVILLE


Then another time we went to Rome and we brought back a beautiful black renaissance plate. Maddalena, the old italian cook, came up to Gertrude Stein's bed-room one morning to bring the water for her bath. Gertrude Stein had the hiccoughs. But cannot the signora stop it, said Maddalena anxiously. No, said Gertrude Stein between hiccoughs. Maddalena shaking her head sadly went away. In a minute there was an awful crash. Up flew Maddalena, oh signora, signora, she said, I was so upset that the signora had the hiccoughs that I broke the black plate that the signora so carefully brought from Rome. Gertrude Stein began to swear, she has a reprehensible habit of swearing whenever anything unexpected happens and she always tells me she learned it in her youth in California, and as I am a loyal Californian I can then say nothing. She swore and the hiccoughs ceased. Maddalena's face was wreathed in smiles. Ah the signorina, she said, she has stopped hiccoughing. Oh no I did not break the beautiful plate, I just made the noise of it and then said I did it to make the signorina stop hiccoughing.

**Gertrude Stein,** THE AUTOBIOGRAPHY OF
ALICE B. TOKLAS


One learns in life to keep silent and draw one's own confusions.

**Cornelia Otis Skinner**


Jennie Churchill, whose house in Great Cumberland Place was exactly opposite ours, felt I had the makings of something, or she would not have given herself so much trouble. Every morning while she breakfasted I had to read aloud to her the leader in *The Times,* and submit to a short political lecture, in order that I might not appear too ignorant when I dined out. How right she was and how well fitted for the part. I was reminded that it was not for my personal amusement that I was invited, but to contribute to the entertainment of a party. I must look amiable even if I felt bored; and even if my neighbours at lunch or dinner were dull I must make the effort tò keep the conversation up to the mark.

**Clare Sheridan, TO THE FOUR WINDS**

The talk ran on herbaceous borders – hens and parochial treats, the roads, the rain. There were shakes of the head over the bad manners of the young people, the deterioration of the servants, the sad state of England. And the old and young people smiled on one another and spent a pleasant afternoon in spite of all; the formidable young people pleased at the friendliness of the old, the formidable old people flattered and grateful at the notice of the young. The unformidable middle-aged people pleased, flattered, and grateful at the notice of either.

**F. M. Mayor, THE RECTOR'S DAUGHTER**

Dorothy, like a good many bad-tempered people, was quick to forgive affronts, so that she could start giving and receiving them again.

**Pamela Hansford Johnson, CORK STREET NEXT TO THE HATTER'S**

What are compliments? They are things you say to people when you don't know what else to say.

**Constance Jones, THE TEN YEARS' AGREEMENT**

'O, but I hate dignity,' cried she carelessly, 'for it is the dullest thing in the world.'

**Fanny Burney, CECILIA**

She blushed like a well-trained sunrise.

**Margaret Halsey, WITH MALICE TOWARD SOME**

The beauty of Lord Curzon's first wife had impressed the Indians. She was the daughter of Mr Joseph Leiter of Chicago. Her mother's twistings of words are worthy of immortality: 'What did I like best in Rome? Why, the Apollo with the bevelled ear, the Dying Alligator and Romeo and Juliet being suckled by the wolf.' She used to say that it was essential to have a *ventre-à-terre* in Paris; also that she had given her decorators *bête noire* to do what they liked; and she thus described her first meeting with her future husband at a costume ball – 'He was dressed in the garbage of a monk and I said to Momma, "Alma Mater, Ecce Homo!"'

**Lady Maud Warrender,** MY FIRST 60 YEARS

When Mrs Corrigan, on her arrival in England, took Mrs George Keppel's house in Grosvenor Street, which she called my little *ventre-à-terre*, (she was famous for her malapropisms) . . .

**Daphne Fielding,** EMERALD AND NANCY

The same raconteur also told me of an *ingénue* who asked her neighbour at dinner: *'Qu'est que c'est qu'un hermaphrodite?'* The embarrassed young Frenchman evaded the truth by answering: *'Oh, c'est quelqu'un qui est ni joli ni laid.'* Some time after this to one of her partners who poured out compliments: *'Comme vous êtes belle, mademoiselle, comme vous êtes belle,'* she replied: *'Mais non, mais non, je vous assure que je suis tout simplement hermaphrodite'!*

**Lady Maud Warrender,** MY FIRST 60 YEARS

Oh I see said the Earl but my own idea is that these things are as piffle before the wind.

**Daisy Ashford,** THE YOUNG VISITERS

# House and Garden

Women hate moving house – like mandrakes, they scream when they're uprooted. One wonders if it is because of the nesting instinct that they get so attached to their houses, or because they generally spend so much more time at home than their husbands do, or because, when they don't have a career to boast about, a beautifully kept house symbolises their particular achievement.

One of the great problems today if you do work, *and* try to run a house, *and* look after a family, is to find time to keep your house even passably clean. To the harrassed career woman Elizabeth Bowen's description of a newly spring-cleaned house (page 128) – so evocative you can almost smell the beeswax – takes on the charm of a period piece. But even in this shining, lovingly cherished room, the dirt is beginning to creep back. Few tasks are more like the labour of Sisyphus than housework, the clean constantly being made dirty so that the dirty may be made clean. Sluts of course know this. What's the point of doing housework today, they reason, when it's all going to be dirtied up by tomorrow? No writer understands this predicament better than Katharine Whitehorn. The article she wrote 'On Shirts', in which she asked, 'Have you ever taken anything out of the clothes basket because it has become relatively the cleaner thing?' is a minor masterpiece.

Pamela Hansford Johnson's family of intellectuals seem to have got their priorities right. Children and animals reduce houses to chaos, so there's no point in fretting over it. One is reminded of Lettice Cooper's remark that she only tidied up her flat when she could no longer get to the bookcase.

A passion for gardening often overtakes women when they are past the age of childbearing. Their children are growing up and need them less and less, but out in the garden there are hundreds of growing things that still need tending and cherishing. Few things equal the ecstasy of going out in the early morning, when the garden is flooded with that peculiarly white light, feeling the cold, wet grass beneath your feet, smelling the dew drying on the lavender, and seeing which of your protégés have come out in the night, a tiger lily opened here, the sudden bright blue blaze of a Morning Glory there. Anne Morrow Lindbergh (page 130) must have been up very early to have observed all those unexpected visitors who regard one's garden as their own.

We also include an enchanting poem from E. J. Scovell about white lilac. There is something particularly beautiful about white flowers; they blend so well with all the shifting shades of green. One thinks of the all-white garden at Sissinghurst – the white roses, lilac, and tobacco plants which smell so sweet and shine so luminously in the garden at night.

The spring cleaning had been thorough. Each washed and polished object stood roundly in the unseeing air. The marble glittered like white sugar; the ivory paint was smoother than ivory. Blue spirit had removed the winter film from the mirrors: now their jet-sharp reflections hurt the eye; they seemed to contain reality. The veneers of cabinets blazed with chestnut light. Upstairs and downstairs, everything smelt of polish; a clean soapy smell came out from behind books. Crisp from the laundry, the inner net curtains stirred over windows reluctantly left open to let in the April air with its faint surcharge of soot. Yet, already, with every breath that passed through the house, pollution was beginning.

**Elizabeth Bowen,** THE DEATH OF THE HEART

As a matter of fact, you know I am rather sorry you should see the garden now, because, alas! it is not looking at its best. Oh, it doesn't compare to what it was last year.

**Ruth Draper,** SHOWING THE GARDEN

The Boultons lived, amid a tangle of children's toys, odd slippers, cats, rubber ducks and plastic chamberpots, in an extremely fine house left to Zena by her father. 'You can't possibly,' she said, kicking something of a vaguely disreputable appearance under the sofa, 'have children and kittens and be smart. Do you know, there are so-called animal experts who recommend removing the cat's claws so that he can't tear the furniture? Good grief! Removing the poor brute's natural means of defence! Anyone who puts furniture before cats and children shouldn't be allowed to have either. Nor any furniture, come to that.'

**Pamela Hansford Johnson,** CORK STREET NEXT TO THE HATTER'S

Those comfortably padded lunatic asylums which are known, euphemistically, as the stately homes of England.

**Virginia Woolf,** THE COMMON READER: LADY DOROTHY NEVILL

It had a lovely white shiny bath and sparkling taps and several towels arranged in readiness by thoughtful Horace. It also had a step for climbing up the bath and other good dodges of a rich nature.

**Daisy Ashford,** THE YOUNG VISITERS

My dear, don't change a thing; it's simply you.

> Attributed to **Anne, Countess of Rosse;** said to an
> aged crone sitting in a turf cabin on a mound of pig-
> dung complaining about the water coming through
> the roof

American interiors tend to have no happy medium between execrable
taste and what is called 'good taste' and is worn like a wart.

> **Margaret Halsey,** WITH MALICE TOWARD SOME

'How wonderful it must have been for the Ancient Britons,' my mother
said once, 'when the Romans arrived and they could have a Hot Bath.'

> **Katharine Whitehorn,** ROUNDABOUT

Untidy is perhaps too mild a word; slut would be a better one. Being a
slut is of course partly a matter of bad luck as well as bad management:
things just do boil over oftener, fuses blow sooner, front doors bang
leaving us outside in our dressing-gowns; but it goes deeper than bad
luck. We are not actually incapable of cleaning our homes: but we are
liable to reorganize instead of scrub; we do our cleaning in a series of
periodic assaults. A mother-in-law has only to appear over the horizon
and we act like the murderer in the Ray Bradbury story who kept on
wiping the finger prints off the fruit at the bottom of the bowl. We work
in a frenzy; but unfortunately the frenzy usually subsides before we
have got everything back into the cupboards again.

> **Ibid**

When you dwell in a house you mislike, you will look out of window a
deal more than those that are content with their dwelling.

> **Mary Webb,** PRECIOUS BANE

The world has different owners at sunrise. Fields belong to hired men opening gates for cows; meadows, to old women with carpet bags, collecting mushrooms. Even your own garden does not belong to you. Rabbits and blackbirds have the lawns; a tortoise-shell cat who never appears in daytime patrols the brick walls, and a golden-tailed pheasant glints his way through the iris spears.

**Anne Morrow Lindbergh,** LISTEN, THE WIND

I only once saw a wood of lilac – more than three
Or four together, light by darker purple massed
In gardens. That wild grove had every stem a tree,
A thicket of white lilac with its loose and tossed
Habit and flowers like surf or flakes of light on sea.

This time of year, the garden lilacs light by dark,
The curtained morning bird-songs inexhaustible
Over the rich gardens, the cuckoo most of all
Emptying the sky of these from heavens beyond the park
Bring to my mind that wood of white lilac run wild;
The birds seem foam-born there, the cuckoo even might build.

**E. J. Scovell,** 'A WOOD OF LILAC'

The kiss of the sun for pardon,
    The song of the birds for mirth,
One is nearer God's Heart in a garden
    Than anywhere else on earth.

**Dorothy Frances Gurney,** 'GOD'S GARDEN'

I don't believe the half I hear
    Nor the quarter of what I see!
But I have one faith, sublime and true,
    That nothing can shake or slay;
Each spring I firmly believe anew
    All the seed catalogues say!

**Caroyln Wells,** 'ONE FIRM FAITH'

O moon, when I gaze on thy beautiful face,
Careering along through the boundaries of space,
The thought has often come into my mind
If I ever shall see thy glorious behind.

**A Housemaid Poet,** quoted by Robert Ross in THE
ACADEMY

# Town and Country

Few subjects move the English more than nature – and women authors are no exception. 'Earth's crammed with heaven,' wrote Elizabeth Barrett Browning, 'and every common bush afire with God.' This awareness makes a poet find beauty in the most unlikely places. The heart of the town-dweller, for example, quickens and rejoices just as much at the first tiny buff leaves of the plane tree as that of the country-dweller, like Dorothy Wordsworth, who is moved to ecstasy by a lakeland wood bowed down with snow (page 136).

Our first extract revives the age-old battle between the countryman and the town-dweller. Both have their justifiable points of view but it is a curious fact that while the countryman is at liberty to express his dislike of the big city the same freedom of expression is seldom allowed the town-dweller. For example, it is perfectly all right for one's cousin from Norfolk to say, 'I can't bear the noise and the smell of London but I've got to come up to see my dressmaker; do you think I could have a bed for a couple of nights?' It is *not* all right, when staying with one's cousin in Norfolk, to say, 'I can't imagine how you can live in this bleak, barren, windswept place. Thank God I'm going back to London today.'

Few birds have been written about more than the cuckoo – Shakespeare, Matthew Arnold, Wordsworth have all sung his praises. But few writers have captured his unrepentant joyous nature better than Rose Macaulay (page 134).

We have three very different descriptions of sheep from Rose Macaulay, Mary Webb and Dorothy Wordsworth. Rose Macaulay's poem is delightful but very conventional, and might easily have been composed in a drawing-room from rosy memory. Both Mary Webb and Dorothy Wordsworth, however, write from familiarity and close observation.

Anyone who has read Dorothy Wordsworth's diaries will realise how great a debt both Wordsworth and Coleridge owed her. To refresh his memory, William would make her read out passages, and we can see how her description of Ullswater (page 136) influenced his famous poem 'I Wandered Lonely as a Cloud'.

Although Vita Sackville-West was well known as a novelist, none of her characters seemed really to come to life. One feels she was far happier evoking the countryside she loved so much. We quote two passages, the first describing sunset across the lake at Sissinghurst, the second from 'The Land' expressing the joy of coming home after being away.

We also particularly liked Eleanour Sinclair Rohde's piece about the evening primrose (page 138). Miss Rohde beautifully describes how with the coming of night when we can no longer *see* the beauties of nature so clearly our other senses are heightened and we become far more aware of the scent of the flowers and the music of the trees.

'But isn't London a tremendous grand city?'

'So Londoners do say, whatever.'

'But what is it like, Tom dear?'

'Bigger and richer and wickeder than those ungodly cities of old mentioned in the Bible. Londoners be terrible proud of that. There's a tidy few churches and chapels in it too, but not much religion, I should say. Londoners be as queer a lot as ever I saw. Terrible sharp and quick in their ways, and speaking a awful low comical kind o' English – 'tis a wonder they can understand one another at all.'

'But London town itself,' Nell persisted, 'what did you think o' that?'

'Well, I weren't there more'n a two-three nights and then mostly about the Smithfield. They eat their meat disgusting raw in them foreign parts, not cooked brown and dry like we'd have it. But that's how the gentry do fancy their meat brought to table, I've heard tell, as though there weren't no such thing as an oven atween the slaughter house and the parlour.'

**Hilda Vaughan,** HER FATHER'S HOUSE

The chestnut's proud, and the lilac's pretty
   The poplar's gentle and tall,
But the plane tree's kind to the poor dull city –
   I love him best of all!

**Edith Nesbit,** 'CHILD'S SONG IN SPRING'

The rounded buses look through softest blue,
The pavement smells of dust but of narcissus too,
The awnings stretch like petals in the sun,
And even the oldest taxis glitter as they run.

Over the sooted secret garden walls,
As in another Eden cherry-blossom falls,
Lithe under shadowing lilac steal the cats,
And even the oldest ladies tilt their summery hats.

**Frances Cornford,** 'LONDON SPRING'

And then, from the brown heart of Roundabout Copse, breaks the cry, high, far and clear, of the roving bully who is just arrived for his season of pleasure and increase in these islands after his African tour, and carelessly brags the freedom of himself and spouse from household cares, from the tedium of domesticity, from the trouble of parenthood, from the monotony of monogamy. The cuckoo is a witty bird; hearing his gay, cool, exultant cry, one hails once more the eternal pleasurist. They know how to live, these cuckoos; they rove, they love (briefly, but effectively), they breed, they procreate, they lay their cheerful Easter eggs singly in homes of eggs like-hued, relying, with a confidence justified by the inherited experience of ages, on the frail intellects and kind hearts of non-cuculan birds; and so away to the greenwood they hie, having thus made ample and painless provision for a progeny they have no notion of ever seeing again. Family business thus brilliantly disposed of, all spring and summer stretches before them for song, riot and debauchery; and why in the world their name has been taken by humanity as a synonym for stupidity, passes conjecture. Wise birds; intelligent, unscrupulous, cynical, sensible birds, wearing their freedom like a panache, crying it like a witty brag. They seem to me to have a Renaissance touch, to be like Medici princes and popes, luxurious, clever, conscienceless, getting the better of simpler, better men and women, looting the world of its pleasures and giving in return only their own insolent enjoyment. Life is no trouble to cuckoos; *solvitur cantando.* Their gay boast rings over the April woods like bells ringing in the merry summer.

**Rose Macaulay,** PERSONAL PLEASURES

In fact, it is about five o'clock in an evening that the first hour of spring strikes – autumn arrives in the early morning, but spring at the close of a winter day. The air, about to darken, quickens and is run through with mysterious white light; the curtain of darkness is suspended, as though for some unprecedented event. There is perhaps no sunset, the trees are not yet budding – but the senses receive an intimation, an intimation so fine, yet striking in so directly, that this appears a movement in one's own spirit. This exalts whatever feeling is in the heart.

No moment in human experience approaches in its intensity this experience of the solitary earth's. The later phases of spring, when her foot is in at the door, are met with a conventional gaiety. But her first unavowed presence is disconcerting: silences fall in company – the wish to be either alone or with a lover is avowed by some look or some spontaneous movement – the window being thrown open, the glance away up the street. In cities the traffic lightens and quickens; even buildings take such feeling of depth that the streets might be rides cut through a wood. What is happening is only acknowledged between strangers, by looks, or between lovers. Unwritten poetry twists the hearts of people in their thirties. To the person out walking that first evening of spring, nothing appears inanimate, nothing not sentient: darkening chimneys, viaducts, villas, glass-and-steel factories, chain stores seem to strike as deep as natural rocks, seem not only to exist but to dream. Atoms of light quiver between the branches of stretching-up black trees. It is in this unearthly first hour of spring twilight that earth's almost agonised livingness is most felt. This hour is so dreadful to some people that they hurry indoors and turn on the lights – they are pursued by the scent of violets sold on the kerb.

> **Elizabeth Bowen, THE DEATH OF THE HEART**

In such a Night, when passing Clouds give place,
Or thinly vail the Heav'n's mysterious Face;
When in some River, overhung with Green,
The waving Moon and trembling Leaves are seen;
When freshen'd Grass now bears it self upright,
And makes cool Banks to pleasing Rest invite,
Whence springs the Woodbind, and the Bramble-Rose,
And where the sleepy Cowslip shelter'd grows;
Whilst now a paler hue the Foxglove takes,
Yet checquers still with Red the dusky brakes;
When scatter'd Glow-worms, but in Twilight fine,
Shew trivial Beauties watch their Hour to shine;

> **Anne Finch, Countess of Winchilsea, 'A NOCTURNAL REVERIE'**

I never saw daffodils so beautiful; they grew among the mossy stones about and about them, some rested their heads upon these stones as on a pillow for weariness and the rest tossed and reeled and danced and seemed as if they verily laughed with the wind that blew upon them over the lake, they looked so gay ever glancing ever changing. This wind blew directly over the lake to them. There was here and there a little knot and a few stragglers a few yards higher up but they were so few as not to disturb the simplicity and unity and life of that one busy highway.

> **Dorothy Wordsworth, JOURNALS**

A deep snow upon the ground. Wm and Coleridge walked to Mr Bartholemew's. Wm returned, and we walked through the wood into the Coombe to fetch some eggs. The sun shone bright and clear. A deep stillness in the thickest part of the wood, undisturbed except by the occasional dropping of the snow from the holly boughs; no other sound but that of the water, and the slender notes of a redbreast, which sang at intervals on the outskirts of the southern side of the wood. There the bright green moss was bare at the roots of the trees, and the little birds were upon it. The whole appearance of the wood was enchanting; and each tree, taken singly, was beautiful. The branches of the hollies pendent with their white burden, but still showing their bright red berries, and their glossy green leaves. The bare branches of the oaks thickened by the snow.

**Ibid**

We rose early. A thick fog obscured the distant prospect entirely, but the shapes of the nearer trees and the dome of the wood dimly seen and dilated. It cleared away between ten and eleven. The shapes of the mist, slowly moving along, exquisitely beautiful; passing over the sheep they almost seemed to have more of life than those quiet creatures. The unseen birds singing in the mist.

**Ibid**

The wide tides of gold surge, quiet and cold;
    The green west turns deep blue;
The moon's worn slip very soon will dip,
    Like a pale night-bird from view.
There seems no sound in the world all round
    But of horn feet and quavering cries
In the young cold hour . . . Like flame, like a flower
    The sun springs, huge with surprise.

**Rose Macaulay, 'Driving Sheep'**

Deborah and her father returned through the hill gate, going by tracks that ran above steep cwms where threads of water made a small song and the sheep clung half-way up like white flies; past the high springs where water soaked out among the mimulus to feed the rivers of the plain; up slopes of trackless hills, through wet wimberries; across the great plateaux – purple in the rainy light – that stretched in confused vistas on every side, familiar to John as air to a swallow. They passed the small white signpost that rose from the midst of the westward table-land, as others rose from various lost points in the vast expanses – shepherds' signposts, pointing vaguely down vague ways, sometimes directing people dispassionately between two paths, as if it mattered little which they chose.

**Mary Webb, The Golden Arrow**

Notice, and am gratified by, appearance of large clump of crocuses near the front gate. Should like to make whimsical and charming references to these, and try to fancy myself as 'Elizabeth of the German Garden' but am interrupted by Cook, saying that the Fish is here, but he's only brought cod and haddock, and the haddock doesn't smell any too fresh, so what about cod?

Have often noticed that Life is like that.

E. M. Delafield, DIARY OF A PROVINCIAL LADY

Not soon shall I forget – a sheet
Of golden water, cold and sweet,
The young moon with her head in veils
Of silver, and the nightingales.

A wain of hay came up the lane –
O fields I shall not walk again,
And trees I shall not see, so still
Against a sky of daffodil!

Fields where my happy heart had rest,
And where my heart was heaviest,
I shall remember them at peace
Drenched in moon-silver like a fleece.

Katharine Tynan, 'FAREWELL'

Oh why do you walk through the fields in gloves
    Missing so much and so much?
Oh fat white woman who nobody loves,
Why do you walk through the field in gloves
When the grass is as soft as the breast of doves
    And shivering-sweet to the touch?
Oh why do you walk through the fields in gloves
    Missing so much and so much?

Frances Cornford, 'To a Fat Lady seen from the Train'

No evening scents, I think, have the fascination of the delicate fragrance of the evening primroses, especially that of the commonest variety. Those pale moons irradiate the twilight with their sweet elusive perfumes. Like the flowers themselves their scent as night draws in becomes full of mystery and holds an imagination captive. And the scent of limes, what an exquisite scent that is – as exquisite as the music of the trees. To me the loveliest music in the world is the music of the evening breeze in the lime trees on a July evening. Each one of us, I suppose, dreams their own dreams and reads their own thoughts in the wondrously varied music of the trees. Just as with the music of bells. 'He that hears bells will make them sound what he list; as the soul thinketh, so the bell clinketh.' The sound of the wind among the beeches is a glorious sound, deep, rich and full. It is magnificent, but it is of this earth. The music of limes is a far-away melody reaching to the stars, a music which sweeps our thoughts to those stupendous flowers set by Almighty God in the gardens of space.

**Eleanour Sinclair Rohde,** THE SCENTED GARDEN

I like trees because they seem more resigned to the way they have to live than other things do.

**Willa Cather,** O PIONEERS

Look! Where the willows hide a rushing pool.
And the old horse goes squelching down to cool,
One angler's rod against their silvery green,
Still seen to-day as once by Bewick seen.

**Frances Cornford,** 'TRAVELLING HOME'

The autumn bonfire smokes across the woods
And reddens in the water of the moat;
As red within the water burns the scythe,
And the moon dwindled to her gibbous tithe
    Follows the sunken sun afloat.
Green is the eastern sky and red the west;
The hop-kilns huddle under pallid hoods;
The waggon stupid stands with upright shaft,
As daily life accepts the night's arrest.
Night like a deeper sea engulfs the land,
The castle, and the meadows, and the farm;
Only the baying watch-dog looks for harm,
And shakes his chain towards the lunar brand.

**Vita Sackville-West,** 'SISSINGHURST'

Silent and slow, from point to point,
With stealthy feet he trod,
And one by one, with ruthless hand,
Put out the lamps of God.
Then down the East triumphantly
He hurled his golden rod.

           Constance Morgan, 'THE SONG OF A TRAMP'

There is a spot, 'mid barren hills,
   Where winter howls, and driving rain;
But, if the dreary tempest chills,
   There is a light that warms again.

The house is old, the trees are bare,
   Moonless above bends twilight's dome;
But what on earth is half so dear,
   So longed for, as the hearth of home?

The mute bird sitting on the stone,
   The dank moss dripping from the wall,
The thorn-trees gaunt, the walks o'ergrown,
   I love them – how I love them all!

        Emily Brontë, 'A LITTLE WHILE, A LITTLE WHILE'

The country habit has me by the heart.
I never hear the sheep-bells in the fold,
Nor see the ungainly heron rise and flap
Over the marsh, nor hear the asprous corn
Clash, as the reapers set the sheaves in shocks
(That like a tented army dream away
The night beneath the moon in silvered fields),
Nor watch the stubborn team of horse and man
Graven upon the skyline, nor regain
The sign-posts on the road towards my home
Bearing familiar names – without a strong
Leaping of recognition; only here
Lies peace after uneasy truancy.

        Vita Sackville-West, 'THE LAND'

No harder lies the newborn head
In this dire valley than in lands
Where the long loamy levels spread
And give themselves into men's hands.

Fairer the trustful slumber seems
Beneath the hanging precipice,
Or the eternal-plunging streams
That thunder from the field of ice:

And destined to that dreadful sea,
Or the lean, little field that lies
Under the heel of tempest, he
Is master of their mysteries

Ruth Pitter, 'THE MOUNTAINOUS COUNTRY'

# Faith ... Diversified by Doubt

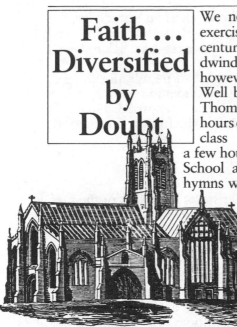

We now turn to religion, a subject that exercises writers less and less as the twentieth century progresses and church attendances dwindle. At the turn of the century, however, nearly everyone went to church. Well brought up country childen, as Flora Thompson points out, were incarcerated for hours even on the finest days; while working-class children, to give their parents a few hours' peace, were dispatched to Sunday School after lunch, and no doubt sang the hymns written by Jane and Ann Taylor (page 145). It seems extraordinary that it took two women to produce such an awesomely frightful poem.

One notices that both Isadora Duncan and Sarah Norcliffe Cleghorn emphasise the essentially communistic nature of Christianity. It is also irritating to find a bohemian like Isadora recanting on art at the last moment (page 147) in favour of universal love. Willa Cather, on the other hand (page 146), utterly disagrees with her.

What is unnerving about the earlier moralists is how much they emphasise the importance of stoicism and passive resignation. Lillian Smith, in a beautiful piece on page 144, preaches that life's uncertainties should be accepted quietly, while the atrocious Mary Baker Eddy, founder of Christian Science, claimed that love divine meets all needs. Meanwhile, all around her, her followers died in childbirth, and had appendices which ruptured and growths which proliferated unchecked.

Perhaps most chilling of all is the extraordinary outpouring from Iulia de Beausobre, which carries loving one's enemies and embracing the torturer's knife to a point of lunatic masochism. The curious becalmed love–hate relationship that can develop between torturer and tortured is, of course, the theme of *Crime and Punishment*.

Stevie Smith, comfortingly down to earth on page 155, has no truck with the merits of martyrdom. Nor would she approve of Edith Olivier (page 148) hankering after the age before the welfare state, when the poor had to rely on the capricious and sporadic benevolence of the rich. Charity is infinitely more satisfying for the giver than the receiver, and most of the poor would prefer a state pension to a basin of gruel from a lady bountiful.

On the whole, though, the women who preached divine acceptance were religious leaders rather than novelists, poets or philosophers, who are inclined to be far more sceptical. Jacquetta Hawkes, for example, on page 151, questions both the obscurantism of the Catholic Church, and the narrow-minded materialism of

Protestantism. Emily Dickinson plainly preferred an ecstatic form of pantheism (page 146), while both Christina Rossetti (page 152) and Elizabeth Barrett Browning noticed that an excess of religion doesn't always make people very Christian.

In moments of crisis, however, most of us still turn to God. Statesmen, for example, often pick some quotation with a stirring moral content that overnight becomes universally known. Churchill, in one of his great broadcasts to the nation in the forties, chose Arthur Clough's poem which ends:

In front the sun climbs slow, how slowly,
But westward, look, the land is bright.

King George VI, in his first Christmas broadcast of the war, quoted a passage by an unknown American writer called Minnie Louise Haskins which we reproduce. Interesting that both he and Churchill chose images of the dawn breaking.

The only men many unmarried women have access to are clergymen and doctors, which perhaps explains why so many congregations today are composed of maiden ladies or widows, fussing over the vicar and inviting the more comely of the curates to supper. So it is no wonder that a novel about a handsome virile-looking bishop who fell in love with a member of his congregation thrilled thousands of women readers at the turn of the century. The bishop's love was returned but, because his interpretation of his faith was stricter than that of his beloved, trouble ensued. In the extract quoted on page 148 they are already scrapping because the bishop refuses to come to dinner to meet her father during Lent.

Religion is often very confusing for childen. We all know of Gladly the Cross Eyed Bear and Pity Mice Implicitly. In the same genre, we end with M. V. Hughes, who tells of her admiration for Christ's perfect manners on the cross.


And I said to the man who stood at the gate of the year: 'Give me a light that I may tread safely into the unknown.' And he replied: 'Go out into the darkness and put your hand into the hand of God. That shall be to you better than light and safer than a known way.' So I went forth, and finding the hand of God, trod gladly into the night. And he led me towards the hills and the breaking of day in the lone east.

**Minnie Louise Haskins, GOD KNOWS*\***


To find the point where hypothesis and fact meet; the delicate equilibrium between dream and reality; the place where fantasy and earthly things are metamorphosed into a work of art, the hour when

---

*Quoted by King George VI in a radio
broadcast to the Empire, 25 December 1939.
At that time the authorship was unknown.

faith in the future becomes knowledge of the past; to lay down one's power for others in need; to shake off the old ordeal and get ready for the new; to question, knowing that never can the full answer be found; to accept uncertainties quietly, even our incomplete knowledge of God; this is what man's journey is about, I think.

**Lillian Smith,** THE JOURNEY

Thanks to St Matthew, who had been
At mass-meetings in Palestine,
We know whose side was spoken for
When Comrade Jesus had the floor.

**Sarah Norcliffe Cleghorn,** 'COMRADE JESUS'

He went about, he was so kind,
To cure poor people who were blind;
And many who were sick and lame,
He pitied them and did the same.

**Ann** and **Jane Taylor,** HYMNS FOR SUNDAY SCHOOLS: ABOUT JESUS CHRIST

I've seen the smiling
Of Fortune beguiling
I've felt all her favours and found her decay;
Sweet was her blessing,
Kind her caressing:
But now they are fled, fled far away.

**Alison Cockburn,** 'THE FLOWERS OF THE FOREST'

Laugh, and the world laughs with you;
Weep, and you weep alone;
For the sad old earth must borrow its mirth,
But has trouble enough of its own.

**Ella Wheeler Wilcox,** 'SOLITUDE'

In Bishop Donaldson's drawing-room at Salisbury a year or two before his death, there was one day a conversation about family prayers. The Bishop asked if many people still had them, and nearly everyone said 'No'. Mrs Buckley was one of the exceptions and she said that one of her reasons for keeping up the practice was that her servants liked it so much.

'In fact,' she went on, 'It's all I can do to prevent my guests from coming too.'

'*Prevent* them from coming?' asked the Bishop astounded.

'Of course. They would make me far too shy.'

**Edith Olivier,** Without Knowing Mr Walkley

The afternoon service with not a prayer left out or a creed spared seemed to the children everlasting. The schoolchildren, under the stern eye of the Manor House, dared not so much as wriggle; they sat in their stiff, stuffy, best clothes, their stomachs lined with heavy Sunday dinner, in a kind of waking doze through which Tom's 'Amens' rang like a bell and the Rector's voice buzzed beelike. Only on the rare occasions when a bat fluttered down from the roof, or a butterfly drifted in at a window, or the Rector's little fox terrier looked in at the door and sidled up to the nave, was the tedium lighted.

**Flora Thompson,** Lark Rise to Candleford

Religion and art spring from the same root and are close kin. Economics and art are strangers.

**Willa Cather,** On Writing

Some keep the Sabbath going to Church;
I keep it staying at home,
With a bobolink for a chorister,
And an orchard for a dome.

**Emily Dickinson***

Dear Lord, the day of eggs is here.

**Amanda M. Ros,** Ode to Easter

---

*Emily Dickinson describes herself in a letter to a friend: 'I . . . am small, like the wren; and my hair is bold like the chestnut burr; and my eyes like the sherry in the glass that the guest leaves.'

Only two of her poems were printed during her lifetime, neither with her consent. After her death her poems were found among her papers and, by a fortunate decision of her sister Lavinia, were preserved and published.

The first idea that the child must acquire, in order to be actively disciplined, is that of the difference between good and evil; and the task of the educator lies in seeing that the child does not confound good with immobility and evil with activity, as often happens in the case of the oldtime discipline. And all this because our aim is to discipline for activity, for work, for good, not for immobility, not for passivity, not for obedience.

**Maria Montessori,** THE MONTESSORI METHOD

Art is not necessary at all. All that is necessary to make this world a better place to live in is to love – to love as Christ loved, as Buddha loved . . . That was the most marvellous thing about Lenin: *he* really loved mankind. Others loved themselves, money theories, power: Lenin loved his fellow men . . . Lenin was God, as Christ was God, because God is Love and Christ and Lenin were all Love!

**Isadora Duncan***

Being is holiness, harmony, immortality. It is already proved that a knowledge of this, even in a small degree, will uplift the physical and moral standard of mortals, will increase longevity, will purify and elevate character. Thus progress will finally destroy all error, and bring immortality to light.

**Mary Baker Eddy,** SCIENCE AND HEALTH**

Divine Love always has met and always will meet every human need.

**Ibid**

*This comes from the first chapter of her memoirs, which she dictated in Berlin in 1924 but never completed. It appeared in the magazine *This Quarter*, Paris, 1929.

**What she has really discovered are ways and means of perverting and prostituting the science of healing to her own ecclesiastical aggrandizement, and to the moral and physical depravity of her dupes.

Mrs Josephine Woodbury,
Quimbyism, or the Paternity of
Christian Science, in ARENA, 1899.

147

We were discussing the possibility of making one of our cats Pope recently, and we decided that the fact that she was not Italian, and was a female, made the third point, that she was a cat, quite irrelevant.

**Katharine Whitehorn**, LUCIAD, Leicester University Magazine, January 1965

The lovely word Charity is out of favour today; and the personal gifts which brightened the days I write of are now looked back on as ugly symptoms of a state of society in which the rich alternately trampled upon and patronized the poor. Yet the unhappy people in those days were those who lived in big towns out of reach of this simple and friendly giving and receiving. In little country places these presents often passed between people whose circumstances were not actually very far apart; and they carried with them a personal friendship which an Income-Tax return cannot convey. The columns of figures which fill out our Rates and Taxes Demand Notes have taken the place of the basins which used to bring dinners from one house to another, and a great deal of flavour is lost in this exchange.

**Edith Olivier**, WITHOUT KNOWING MR WALKLEY

'I don't quite see, Archie,' she said (she had long ago taken to calling him Archie), 'I don't quite see what Lent has to do with your going to a dinner-party.'

'But,' he answered, 'I have never gone out to entertainments during Lent in my life . . .'

'But you want to come, don't you?' she asked.

'Yes, I would like to come, of course I would like to come; but that is the more reason why I should not do so . . .'

'I don't think,' she said thoughtfully, 'that you ought to have engaged yourself to me just before Lent if you meant Lent to interfere with proper attention to me, and it is a proper attention to me that you should meet my friends and my father's friends as my future husband.'

**Eliza Vaughan Stannard**, THE SOUL OF THE BISHOP

A great bond is formed, he says, between the man who is tortured day in, day out, and the man who, day in, day out, tortures him. Greater than there could possibly be between the tortured man and the blithe free citizen who understands nothing because he does not want to see or know a thing. If you ponder on this you may find the justification for your apparently absurd suffering.

But, Leonardo, surely there is no justification for a crowd of well-fed reasonably strong men bullying a weary, under-nourished, half-demented woman who doesn't even know what it is all about . . .

It is unpardonable that anyone should be tortured, even you – if *you* merely leave it at that. But, surely, when you overcome the pain inflicted on you by them, you make *their* criminal record less villainous? Even more – you bring something new into it – a thing of precious beauty. But when, through weakness, cowardice, lack of balance, lack of serenity, you augment your pain, their crime becomes so much the darker, and it is darkened by you. If you could understand this, your making yourself invulnerable would not be only an act of self-preservation; it would be a kindness to *Them* . . . Look down right into the depths of your heart and tell me – Is it not right for you to be kind to them? Even to them? Particularly to them, perhaps? Is it not right that those men who have no kindness in them should get a surplus of it flowing towards them from without? . . . The whole of me responds with a 'Yes!' like a throb of thundering music.

**Iulia de Beausobre**, THE WOMAN WHO COULD NOT DIE

I wish I knew more saints . . . I hardly know a saint . . . Oh, there's St Lawrence with his grill . . . Well, he was broiled as a martyr, dear, and in the pictures he always carries a grill . . . I want to get a postcard of him.

**Ruth Draper**, IN A CHURCH IN ITALY

There are different kinds of wrong. The people sinned against are not always the best.

**Ivy Compton-Burnett**, THE MIGHTY AND THEIR FALL

If sexual experiences were theoretically minimal, social expectations were on the contrary great. Once there was a Drag Hunt Ball just outside Oxford, to which I had unaccountably failed to be asked. I asked God to do something about it, and God recklessly killed poor King George VI, as a result of which the Hunt Ball was cancelled.

**Antonia Fraser**, MY OXFORD

Ah, don't let my prayer seem too little to You, God. You sit up there, so white and old, with all the angels about You and the stars slipping by. And I come to You with a prayer about a telephone call. Ah, don't laugh, God. You see, You don't know how it feels. You're so safe, there on Your throne, with the blue swirling under You. Nothing can touch You; no one can twist Your heart in his hands. This is suffering, God, this is bad, bad suffering.

**Dorothy Parker,** A TELEPHONE CALL

January 25th: Attend a Committee Meeting in the village to discuss how to raise funds for Village Hall. Am asked to take the chair. Begin by saying that I know how much we all have this excellent object at heart, and that I feel sure there will be no lack of suggestions as to best method of obtaining requisite sum of money. Pause for suggestions, which is met with death-like silence. I say, There are so many ways to choose from – implication being that I attribute silence to plethora of ideas, rather than to absence of them. (Note: Curious and rather depressing, to see how frequently the pursuit of GoodWorks leads to apparently unavoidable duplicity.) Silence continues, and I say Well, twice, and Come, come, once. (Sudden impulse to exclaim, 'I lift up my finger and I say Tweet, Tweet,' is fortunately overcome.) At last extract a suggestion of a concert from Mrs L. (whose son plays the violin) and a whist-drive from Miss P. (who won Ladies First Prize at the last one). Florrie P. suggests a dance and is at once reminded that it will be Lent. She says that Lent isn't what it was. Her mother says the Vicar is one that holds with Lent, and always has been. Someone else says That reminds her, has anyone heard that old Mr Small passed away last night? We all agree that eighty-six is a great age. Mrs L. says that on her mother's side of the family, there is an aunt of ninety-eight. Still with us, she adds. The aunt's husband, on the other hand, was gathered just before his sixtieth birthday. Everyone says, You can't ever *tell,* not really. There is a suitable pause before we go back to Lent and the Vicar. General opinion that a concert isn't like a dance, and needn't – says Mrs L. – interfere.

On this understanding, we proceed. Various familiar items – piano solo, recitation, duet, and violin solo from Master L. – are all agreed upon. Someone says that Mrs F. and Miss H. might do a dialogue, and has to be reminded that they are no longer on speaking terms, owing to strange behaviour of Miss H. about her bantams. Ah, says Mrs S., it wasn't only *bantams* was at the bottom of it, there's two sides to every question. (There were at least twenty to this one, by the time we've done with it.)

Sudden appearance of our Vicar's wife, who says apologetically that she made a mistake in the time. I beg her to take the chair. She refuses. I insist. She says No, no, positively not, and takes it. We begin all over again, but general attitude towards Lent much less elastic.

**E. M. Delafield,** DIARY OF A PROVINCIAL LADY

He that will live in this world must be endued with the three rare qualities of dissimulation, equivocation and mental reservation.

**Aphra Behn,** THE ROUNDABOUTS

'Place before your eyes two precepts, and only two. One is Preach the Gospel; and the other is – *Put down enthusiasm!*' . . . The Church of England in a nutshell.

**Mrs Humphry Ward,** ROBERT ELSMERE

The discouragement of radical thought must lead to the closed society and closed mind; and so, too, may our present orthodox forms of Christianity - Catholocism through its liking for ignorance, Protestantism through its approval of moneymaking, respectability, and the whole crowned and mitred body of the status quo.

**Jacquetta Hawkes,** NEW STATESMAN, JANUARY 1957

Religion converts despair, which destroys, into resignation, which submits.

**The Countess of Blessington**

I'll not listen to reason . . . Reason always means what someone else has got to say.

**Mrs Gaskell,** CRANFORD

A clergyman has nothing to do but to be slovenly and selfish – read the newspaper, watch the weather, and quarrel with his wife. His curate does all the work and the business of his own life is to dine.

**Jane Austen,** MANSFIELD PARK

She gave up beauty in her tender youth,
   Gave all her hope and joy and pleasant ways;
   She covered up her eyes lest they should gaze
On vanity, and chose the bitter truth.
Harsh towards herself, towards others full of ruth,
   Servant of servants, little known to praise,
   Long prayers and fasts trenched on her nights and days:
She schooled herself to sights and sounds uncouth
That with the poor and stricken she might make
   A home, until the least of all sufficed
Her wants; her own self learned she to forsake,
Counting all earthly gain but hurt and loss.
So with calm will she chose and bore the cross
   And hated all for love of Jesus Christ.

**Christina Rossetti, 'A PORTRAIT'**


Some people always sigh in thanking God.

**Elizabeth Barrett Browning, 'AURORA LEIGH'**


   Vain are the thousand creeds
That move men's hearts, unutterably vain;
   Worthless as withered weeds
Or idlest froth amid the boundless main.

**Emily Brontë, 'NO COWARD SOUL IS MINE'**


Uncle Matthew went with Aunt Sadie and Linda on one occasion to a Shakespeare play, *Romeo and Juliet*. It was not a success. He cried copiously, and went into a furious rage because it ended badly. 'All the fault of that damned padre,' he kept saying on the way home, still wiping his eyes. 'That fella, what's 'is name, Romeo, might have known a blasted papist would mess up the whole thing. Silly old fool of a nurse too, I bet she was an R.C., dismal old bitch.'

**Nancy Mitford, THE PURSUIT OF LOVE**

After all, His (Christ's) mission has proved scarcely less than a complete failure; two thousand years have passed and Christians do not number one-fifth part of the population of the globe.

**Elena Blavatsky**

She'd give the shirt from off her back, except that
She doesn't wear a shirt, and most men do;
And often and most bitterly she's wept that
A starving tramp can't eat a silver shoe,
Or some poor beggar, slightly alcoholic,
Enjoy with Donne a metaphysical frolic.

**Elinor Wylie, 'PORTRAIT IN BLACK PAINT'**

Men who make no pretensions to being good on one day out of seven are called sinners.

**Mary Wilson Little**

Often devotion to virtue arises from sated desire.

**'Laurence Hope' (Adela Florence Cory Nicolson), 'I ARISE AND GO DOWN TO THE RIVER'**

If you stop to be kind you must swerve often from your path.

**Mary Webb, PRECIOUS BANE**

The fates are not quite obdurate;
    They have a grim, sardonic way
Of granting them who supplicate
    The thing they wanted yesterday.

**Roselle Mercier Montgomery, 'THE FATES'**

The worst and best are both inclined
To snap like vixens at the truth.
But, O, beware the middle mind
That purrs and never shows a tooth!

Elinor Wylie, NONSENSE RHYMES

Lying increases the creative faculties, expands the ego, lessens the friction of social contacts . . . it is only in lies, wholeheartedly and bravely told, that human nature attains through words and speech the forbearance, the nobility, the romance, the idealism, that –being what it is – it falls so short of in fact and in deed.

Clare Boothe Luce, VANITY FAIR, October 1930

Good for the soul – but bad for the heel.

Agnes Guilfoyle (on confession)

Sin has always been an ugly word, but it has been made so in a new sense over the last half-century. It has been made not only ugly but *passé*. People are no longer sinful, they are only immature or underprivileged or frightened or, more particularly, sick.

Phyllis McGinley, THE PROVINCE OF THE HEART: IN DEFENCE OF SIN

My definition (of a philosopher) is of a man up in a balloon, with his family and friends holding the ropes which confine him to earth and trying to haul him down.

Louisa May Alcott, LIFE, LETTERS AND JOURNALS

You have heard me quote from Plato
  A thousand times, no doubt;
Well, I have discovered that he did not know
  What he was talking about.

**Ella Wheeler Wilcox**


Humility is not my forté, and whenever I dwell for any length of time on
my own shortcomings, they gradually begin to seem mild, harmless,
rather engaging little things, not at all like the staring defects in other
people's characters.

**Margaret Halsey, WITH MALICE TOWARD SOME**


People who are always praising the past
And especially the times of faith as best
Ought to go and live in the Middle Ages
And be burnt at the stake as witches and sages.

**Stevie Smith, 'THE PAST'**


Many people of my age must have imbibed their early religious notions
from the same book that I did – *The Peep of Day,* for my copy is dated
1872, and is one of the three hundred and forty-seventh thousand. It is
very insistent and realistic about hell, and apparently there is only one
virtue, obedience to parents and kind teachers, which leads of itself to a
life of bliss 'beyond the sky'. One stanza of verse attracted me greatly:

Satan is glad – when I am bad
And hopes that I – with him shall lie
In fire and chains – and dreadful pains.

Whether the rhythm pleased me, or whether I was gratified that
such an important person as Satan would actually welcome my
company, I can't say, but the idea was more exciting than that of
heaven put forth by the author. The stories about Jesus I liked best, and
admired Him greatly. What a pity, I thought, that after such a good life
He should have told an untruth at last. This is what I read: 'Jesus just
tasted the vinegar and said, "It is finished."' My idea was that He had
been given this horrid stuff to drink, tasted it, and then out of politeness
pretended that he had finished it up.

**M. V. Hughes, A LONDON CHILD OF THE 1870s**

# Culture in Bands

'Life cannot defeat a writer who is in love with writing,' said Edna Ferber, 'for life itself is a writer's lover until death.' In some ways, therefore, writers are insulated against the horrors of the world, for they are usually buoyed up by the feeling that, however terrible an experience, it can be drawn on as capital later.

In this section women talk about writing and the arts generally. Harriet Beecher Stowe, for example, confesses that she had no literary technique when she wrote *Uncle Tom's Cabin*, merely a sense of injustice so powerful that it overflowed on to the page. But she produced only one great book. Pearl Buck and Edith Sitwell agree that a writer will be greater if she is not motivated merely by oppression and a desire to reform the world. Committed writers usually cease to be interesting once the cause they espouse loses its urgency. Ellen Glasgow and Willa Cather complain of the difficulty of finding anything new to say, while Rose Macaulay, who was so good at creating flesh-and-blood characters, is refreshingly dismissive about the importance these characters played in her writing life (page 162).

Most of us are jealous of those who succeed in our own field, particularly if they are of the same sex. Charlotte Brontë, for example, disliked Jane Austen's novels exceedingly. 'Miss Austen,' she wrote, 'being without poetry, maybe is sensible, real (more real than true) but she can never be great.' Dorothy Parker is equally scathing about Margot Asquith in particular and lady novelists in general. Perhaps if she had had the stamina to finish a novel herself, she might have been more tolerant.

Edith Sitwell on page 158 describes a sixteenth-century performance of *Romeo and Juliet*. It is interesting to compare the appalling manners of the rabble in Shakespeare's day with the polite, if bewildered, reverence of a late twentieth-century audience described by Pamela Hansford Johnson in the last book of her Dorothy Merlin trilogy (page 160).

Mrs Ballinger is one of the ladies who pursue Culture in bands, as though it were dangerous to meet it alone.

**Edith Wharton,** Xingu

'. . . But Shakespeare one gets acquainted with without knowing how. It is a part of an Englishman's constitution. His thoughts and beauties are so spread abroad that one touches them everywhere, one is intimate with him by instinct. – No man of any brain can open at a good part of one of his plays, without falling into the flow of his meaning immediately.'

Jane Austen, MANSFIELD PARK

Through all the shrines (at Stratford-on-Avon) surge English and American tourists, either people who have read too much Shakespeare at the expense of good, healthy detective stories or people who have never read him at all and hope to get the same results by bumping their heads on low beams.

All of Stratford, in fact, suggests powdered history – add hot water and stir and you have a delicious, nourishing Shakespeare.

Margaret Halsey, WITH MALICE TOWARD SOME

The play continued, though, when Romeo left the stage after killing Tybalt, he stood in the wings and shook his sword at the box from which the cock had been thrown on to the stage, with the result that the occupants of the box yelled that he must apologize for shaking his sword. Mr Coates, very naturally, refused to do so, and the interruptions continued until the occupants of the pit turned on the interrupters and pelted them with orange peel. The play continued, then, without any further interruption until the moment came when Romeo kills Paris. Then the latter, lying dead upon the ground, was raised to life by 'a terrific blow on the nose from an orange'. The corpse rose to his feet and, pointing in a dignified way to the cause of his revival, made his way off the stage. Mr Coates, we are told was 'considerably annoyed' during the Tomb Scene, by shouts of 'Why don't you die?'

Edith Sitwell, THE ENGLISH ECCENTRICS

Playing Shakespeare is very tiring. You never get to sit down unless you're a King.

Josephine Hull

At the beginning of the nineteenth century the child actor Betty, the 'Infant Roscius', made such a lucrative impact on the public that the stage became infested with a multiplicity of diminutive prodigies, causing the actress Mrs Jordan (mistress of the Duke of Clarence, later King William IV) to exclaim, 'Oh, for the days of King Herod!'

Mrs Matthews, ANECDOTES OF ACTORS

They are silly. They asked me if I'd mind having a slight moustache in this film – and I've got one anyhow.

Irene Handl (quoted in Edward Marsh, AMBROSIA AND SMALL BEER)

I mean, the question actors most often get asked is how they can bear saying the same things over and over again night after night, but God knows the answer to that is, don't we all anyway; might as well get paid for it.

Elaine Dundy, THE DUD AVOCADO

The legend relates that one afternoon while Adam was asleep, Eve, anticipating the Great God Pan, bored some holes in a hollow reed and began to do what is called 'pick out a tune'. Thereupon Adam spoke: 'Stop that horrible noise,' he roared, adding, after a pause, 'besides which, if anyone's going to make it, it's not you but me!'

Dame Ethel Smyth, FEMALE PIPINGS IN EDEN

Dorothy Parker gave a party one night at the Algonquin, and guest Tallulah Bankhead, slightly inebriated, carried on in a wild, indecorous manner. After Miss Bankhead had been escorted out, Mrs Parker called in from an adjoining room, 'Has Whistler's Mother left yet?'

The next day at lunch Tallulah took out a pocket mirror, examined herself painfully, and said, with a glance at Mrs Parker, 'The less I behave like Whistler's Mother the night before, the more I look like her the morning after.'

Robert E. Drennan, WIT'S END

You ask my opinion about taking the young Salzburg musician (Mozart) into your service. I do not know where you can place him, since I feel that you do not require a composer, or other useless people. But if it would give you pleasure, I have no wish to prevent you. What I say here is only meant to persuade you not to load yourself down with people who are useless, and to urge you not to give such people the right to represent themselves as being in your service. It gives one's service a bad name when such types run about like beggars; besides he has a large family.

**The Empress Maria Theresa**, LETTER TO THE ARCHDUKE FERDINAND

What strange impulse is it which induces otherwise trustful people to say they like music when they do not, and thus expose themselves to hours of boredom?

**Agnes Repplier**, UNDER DISPUTE

Nobody really sings in an opera – they just make loud noises.

**Amelita Galli-Curci**

'I say,' he whispered ingenuously to Dorothy, half way through the third act, 'isn't it awful?'

She started, then gave him a smile of brilliant estrangement. He realized that they were by no means thinking as one.

The play concerned three psychopathic siblings who lived with their old mother, who was deaf and dumb, in a suburb of Basildon New Town. They had taken as a lodger a psychopathic prostitute of Lesbian tendencies, with whom they felt themselves in sympathy; but she, whose trouble was gerontophilia, had a fancy for the old lady. At the end of act two she had fought with her – since her advances did not appear to be returned – had heaved her out of her wheel-chair on to the scullery floor and beaten her to death with an Indian club, partly in view of the audience but mostly, to be just, behind a dismantled gas-stove. The denouement would, apparently, deal with the question of whether the siblings should conspire to take the blame for the murder if the prostitute would agree to distribute her ambiguous favours between them, *privatim et seriatim*, before they rang 999. Since all three siblings had always wanted to be hanged, each took a ritual jab at the corpse with a bread-knife to ensure this pleasurable outcome.

They were busy arguing it out; the audience, which had a large admixture of clergymen and elderly ladies, was laughing obediently away with a puzzled expression on its collective face.

'But it's so true,' Dorothy whispered in return, relenting a little since she was his guest, 'it is so inconceivably *true!*'

> **Pamela Hansford Johnson,** Cork Street Next to the Hatter's

I no more thought of style or literary excellence than the mother who rushes into the street and cries for help to save her children from a burning house thinks of the teachings of the rhetorician or the elocutionist.

> **Harriet Beecher Stowe,** on herself, in Forrest Wilson, Crusader in Crinoline*

I have observed with wonder so many intellectual and literary fashions that I have come at last to rely positively upon one conviction alone. No idea is so antiquated that it was not once modern. No idea is so modern that it will not some day be antiquated . . . To seize the flying thought before it escapes us is our only touch with reality.

> **Ellen Glasgow,** Address to the Modern Language Association, 1936

Be born anywhere, little embryo novelist, but do not be born under the shadow of a great creed, not under the burden of original sin, not under the doom of salvation. Go out and be born among gypsies or thieves or among happy workaday people who live in the sun and do not think about their souls.

> **Pearl S. Buck,** Advice to Unborn Novelists

---

*We have seen an American woman write a novel of which a million copies were sold in all languages, and which had one merit, that of speaking to the universal heart, and was read with equal interest to three audiences, namely in the parlour, in the kitchen, and in the nursery of every house.

> **Ralph Waldo Emerson** on Uncle Tom's Cabin in Society and Solitude, Success

The revolt against individualism naturally calls artists severely to account, because the artist is of all men the most individual: those who were not have been long forgotten. The condition every art requires is, not so much freedom from restriction, as freedom from adulteration and from the intrusion of foreign matter, considerations and purposes which have nothing to do with spontaneous invention.

**Willa Cather,** On Writing

I have heard novelists complain that their characters run away with their books and do what they like with them. This must be somewhat disconcerting, like driving an omnibus whose steering-wheel, accelerator and brake are liable to be seized by the passengers. My passengers know their places, and that they are there to afford me the art and pleasure of driving. Are there not, for that matter, already enough people in the world, without these beings intruded from my imagination? Shall they puff themselves up because they are allowed on paper? I have heard of novelists who say that, while they are creating a novel, the people in it are ever with them, accompanying them on walks, for all I know on drives (though this must be distracting in traffic), to the bath, to bed itself. This must be a terrible experience; rather than allow the people in my novels to worry me like that, I should give up writing novels altogether. No; my people are retiring, elusive, and apt not to come even when I require them. I do not blame them. They no doubt wish that they were the slaves of a more ardent novelist, who would permit them to live with her. To be regarded as of less importance than the etymology and development of the meanest word in the dictionary must be galling.

**Rose Macaulay,** Personal Pleasures

Conveying truth by means of fantasy, enlarging our perception of life by poetic means, is one of the highest functions of art, and it is not extravagant to say that in her small and special sphere Beatrix Potter performed it. She understood and loved the little animals that she drew and painted, and perceiving – perhaps without even being aware, for her response to imaginative stimulus was most innocent and direct – perceiving that invisible thread of sympathy which runs through the whole animal creation, including man, she interprets her animals in human terms.

**Margaret Lane,** The Tale of Beatrix Potter

I do not see why exposition and description are a necessary part of a novel. They are not of a play, and both deal with imaginary human beings and their lives. I have been told that I ought to write plays, but cannot see myself making the transition. I read plays with especial pleasure, and in reading novels I am disappointed if a scene is carried through in the voice of the author rather than the voices of the characters. I think that I simply follow my natural bent.

**Ivy Compton-Burnett,** ORION, 1945

Women's poetry should, above all things, be elegant as a peacock, and there should be a fantastic element, a certain strangeness in its beauty. But above all, let us avoid sentimentality: do not let us write about Pierrot, or Arcady, or how much good we should like to do in the world!

**Edith Sitwell,** 'SOME OBSERVATIONS ON WOMEN'S POETRY', VOGUE, 1925

A young Apollo, golden-haired,
  Stands dreaming on the verge of strife,
Magnificently unprepared
  For the long littleness of life.

**Frances Cornford** (on Rupert Brooke)

Surely the excellence of all poetry – what puts Shelley above Keats, Goethe above Shelley (in his lyrics), and English, German and Italian poetry so incomparably above French – surely the great thing is the co-ordination into a total mood, as distinguished from the charm of detached metaphors or descriptions or verses.

**Vernon Lee,** LETTER TO MAURICE BARING

The moment an audacious head is lifted one inch above the general level, pop! goes the unerring rifle of some biographical sharpshooter, and it is all over with the unhappy owner.

**Mary Abigail Dodge,** SKIRMISHES AND SKETCHES

I disapprove so entirely of the plan of writing notices or memoirs of living people, that I must send you on the answer I have already sent to many others; namely an entire refusal to sanction what is to me so objectionable and indelicate a practice by furnishing a single fact with regard to myself. I do not see why the public have any more to do with me than to buy or reject the wares I supply to them.

        **Mrs Gaskell** to a fan

It seems to me much better to read a man's own writing than to read what others say about him, especially when the man is first-rate and the 'others' are third-rate.

        **George Eliot**, LIFE AND LETTERS

'Lord Byron' was an Englishman
    A poet I believe,
His first works in old England
    Was poorly received.
Perhaps it was 'Lord Byron's' fault
    And perhaps it was not.
His life was full of misfortunes,
    Ah, strange was his lot.

        **Julia A. Moore**, 'SKETCH OF LORD BYRON'S LIFE'*

There is a great deal of prose licence in Walt Whitman's poetry.

        **Mary Wilson Little**

---

*Julia Moore was known as 'The Sweet Singer of Michigan'. The Sweet Singer's verse is concerned to a very large extent with total abstinence and violent death, –the great Chicago fire, the railway disaster at Ashtabula, the Civil War, the yellow fever epidemic in the South. She sings death by drowning, by fits, accidents, by lightning-strokes and sleigh. 'Julia is worse than a Gatling gun,' wrote Bill Nye; 'I have counted twenty-one killed and nine wounded in the small volume she has given to the public. She also greatly relishes normal infant mortality, especially in cases where the little victim possesses blue eyes and curling golden hair.'

    From THE STUFFED OWL, selected and arranged by **D. B. Wyndham Lewis** and **Charles Lee**

It always makes me cross when Max (Beerbohm) is called 'The Incomparable Max'. He is not incomparable at all, and in fact compares very poorly with Harold Nicolson, as a stylist, as a wit, and an observer of human nature. He is a shallow, affected, self-conscious fribble – so there.

**Vita Sackville-West,** LETTER TO HAROLD NICOLSON, 9 DECEMBER 1959

'It's Tom's thesis,' said Deirdre in a reverent tone. 'He's just given me a copy to read. Look,' she unwrapped the paper, 'four hundred and ninety-seven pages. How does he do it?'

'Well,' said Catherine, 'writers of fiction would tell you that one just goes on and on until one reaches page four hundred and ninety-seven, but of course we don't have to write at such prodigious length and might well find it a bit of an endurance test. A thesis must be long. The object, you see, is to bore and stupefy the examiners to such an extent that they will have to accept it – only if a thesis is short enough to be read all through word for word is there any danger of failure.'

**Barbara Pym,** LESS THAN ANGELS

'I sent Flora's copy by post,' he said. 'I know she won't read it. She never does. And she always has the same technique of getting out of it. It's amusing to observe. She manages for a while, by acknowledging the book the very moment she receives it; sits down and writes the letter before she could have had a chance to begin the first chapter. "I shall enjoy reading it, and, oh, the pleasure of having it at last, after the anticipation." And so on. Then she keeps well out of my way, until some reviews have appeared, so that she has a phrase or two to tag onto it, or something unfavourable to be indignant at. "*How rude!*" she says. "How *terribly* rude!" Once, I met her by chance, before she was ready for me, and she said that she was taking the book in tiny sips, à petites doses, as Henry James wrote when he was up to the same trick – as if it were the most precious wine. That meant that she was bogged down in it.'

**Elizabeth Taylor,** THE SOUL OF KINDNESS

If there were no such bird as a stormy petrel, those two words would spring together to describe Elinor Wylie. Her appearance was beautiful, brittle and tragic, like *The Venetian Glass Nephew* of whom she wrote, and she was extremely touchy. She was also the most egotistical person I ever knew; but egotism, if joined to intelligence, gives great point to conversation. Elinor's talk was always exciting, because one never knew when she would fly at a tangent into a sudden fury, or quarrel most violently with someone with whom she had, a moment before, been conversing serenely on some high literary topic. I remember one such instantaneous squall when she and Harold Acton were discussing Shelley's poetry. My attention wandered for a moment and then I heard them screaming at each other like fish-wives. She shrieked at him that Roman Catholics never read the Bible, and he hurled back at her that Shelley's face was covered with spots. I never learned how these two poisoned darts came to fit each other as the appropriate ripostes, but they certainly both struck home and roused their opponent to fury.

**Edith Olivier,** WITHOUT KNOWING MR WALKLEY

The affair between Margot Asquith and Margot Asquith will live as one of the prettiest love stories in all literature.

**Dorothy Parker,** review in THE NEW YORKER of THE AUTOBIOGRAPHY OF MARGOT ASQUITH

I don't care what is written about me so long as it isn't true.

**Katharine Hepburn,** 24 APRIL 1954

The books we think we ought to read are poky, dull and dry,
The books that we would like to read we are ashamed to buy;
The books that people talk about we never can recall;
And the books that people give us, Oh, they're the worst of all.

**Carolyn Wells,** 'ON BOOKS'

While Christmas shopping, I asked a pretty college freshman in our local bookstore during the holiday rush for a copy of Dickens' *Christmas Carol*. Smiling sweetly she said, 'Oh, he didn't write songs – he wrote books.'

**Annabel Cowan**

There are only two or three human stories, and they go on repeating themselves as fiercely as if they had never happened before.

**Willa Cather,** O Pioneers!

Yes, I've read all your books. No, I haven't got them. I got them out of the library. They didn't actually have them, but they got them for me. Well, I think it's your honesty I admire so much. You know, the way you use rude words and that.

**Joyce Grenfell,** Stately as a Galleon

I ask if he has published anything lately. He says that his work is not, and never can be, for publication. Thought passes through my mind to the effect that this attitude might with advantage be adopted by many others.

**E. M. Delafield,** Diary of a Provincial Lady

It's really very difficult to describe my grandmother. She wasn't particularly patrician but she did look very like the great Duke of Wellington, only rather prettier. Just as well, really. You know, there is a picture of her in the front of my new book. I don't know – have you read my book, Mr Wimble? No, I know it is so difficult to find time to read what one really wants to. No, it was only since you have so kindly invited me to come on to your television programme in order to discuss my book I thought – you know – that you might just possibly have read it. But I do know how it is.

**Joyce Grenfell,** Stately as a Galleon

A person who publishes a book wilfully appears before the public with his pants down.

**Edna St Vincent Millay**

The only 'ism she believes in is plagiarism

**Dorothy Parker,** of a well-known writer

As artists they're rot, but as providers they're oil wells – they gush.

**Dorothy Parker,** on lady novelists

Some of the new books are so down to earth they ought to be ploughed under.

**Anne Herbert**

In my youth people talked about Ruskin; now they talk about drains.

**Mrs Humphry Ward,** ROBERT ELSMERE

I have the conviction that excessive literary production is a social offence.

**George Eliot**

Aren't the artists brave to go out and paint a sea as rough as that? . . . I don't see how he kept his canvas dry.

**Ruth Draper,** AT AN ART EXHIBITION IN BOSTON

Behind us hung a Correggio St Sebastian, with the usual Buchmanite expression on his face.

'Awful tripe,' said Uncle Matthew, 'fella wouldn't be grinning, he'd be dead with all those arrows in him.'

On the opposite wall was the Montdore Botticelli which Uncle Matthew said he wouldn't give 7s. 6d. for, and when Davey showed him a Leonardo drawing he said his fingers only itched for an india-rubber.

'I saw a picture once,' he said, 'of shire horses in the snow. There was nothing else, just a bit of broken down fence and three horses. It was dangerous good – Army and Navy. If I'd been a rich man I'd have bought that – I mean you could see how cold those poor brutes must have felt. If all this rubbish is supposed to be valuable, that must be worth a fortune.'

**Nancy Mitford,** LOVE IN A COLD CLIMATE

# Mrs Crankhurst

Someone once said that the most ludicrous line he'd ever heard in a film was when an army leader turned to a lot of depressed-looking soldiers in armour and cried out: 'Men of the Middle Ages, let us go forth and fight the Hundred Years' War.'

In the same way it is very difficult for us today to gauge how far or how much further the battle for Women's Liberation will go. Women no longer agree in church to obey their husbands, firms advertise for Persons Friday, pay is supposedly equal and role-reversed husbands often do all the cooking for dinner parties. But a backlash does now seem to be in evidence. Recently the *Daily Mirror* reported a tendency for men to be more chivalrous towards women; a judge refused maintenance to the mother of an illegitimate child who had refused to take the pill, and at a New York production of *The Taming of the Shrew* (which must be the last word in male dominance) hardened feminists, interviewed after the performance, had to admit that it was 'absolutely disgusting, but *so* romantic'. But, as women take over men's roles, men are undoubtedly getting less masculine. 'We've lost more men to homosexuality', moaned Erica Jong, 'than we ever did in two world wars.'

At the start of this section, Marina Warner draws our attention to two fourteenth-century handbooks which urged women to obey their husbands as a religious duty. In those days Patient Griselda, enduring countless humiliations from her husband in order to test her chastity, was the model all good wives were supposed to emulate. Griselda is not unlike the Angel, described by Virginia Woolf (page 176), who inhabited every Victorian household and who was endlessly self-sacrificing and compliant with her husband's wishes.

Despite the passivity of these Angels, throughout the second half of the nineteenth century the women's movement was slowly gathering force, and those young women of the highest intellect portrayed by Isak Dinesen (page 172) were 'coming out of the chiaroscuro of a thousand years, blinking at the sun and wild with desire to test their wings'.

From this first feminist wave, we quote Mrs Pankhurst (page 177) explaining what finally drove her into the movement, and later advocating violence as the only way to achieve her ends. Millicent Fawcett, on the other hand, deplored such methods.

The second feminist wave, that of the post-war years, is represented by Betty Friedan. The extract from *The Feminine Mystique* shows how American women, many of them with degrees, rejected careers as unfeminine, but in a desperate desire for achievement raised domesticity, cooking and motherhood to an art form. Alva Myrdal and Viola Klein (page 175) believe men glorified this cult of motherhood and domesticity in order to assure themselves the cheapest housekeepers in the world. Even Miss Barbara Cartland, famous for the chauvinism of her heroes, allows one of her heroines to complain of the restrictions of being a woman.

The thing that irritates feminists most of all, however, is the number of women who seem to have no desire to be liberated. They have no wish to make all the decisions, or to have to think about money or earning a living. They relish the power that a woman, particularly a pretty one, can have over the male, and how she can use her sexuality as a weapon to get what she wants (Elizabeth Gould Davis, page 176). Germaine Greer, perhaps the most influential figure in the whole movement, expresses her fury that a large bust prevents a woman being taken seriously by men. One is reminded of Madame Armand, one of the great Parisian hostesses of Proust's day, who advised a young wife against starting her own salon by saying:

'You have too luscious a bosom to keep the conversation general.'

Women, as Virginia Woolf explains on page 179, have dedicated themselves over the centuries to making men feel important and clever. 'Plain women', wrote Virginia Graham, 'should know a little bit more than pretty ones and downright ugly ones just a bit more still, but no woman, whatever her physiognomy, should know more than a man – that is if she wants to be loved by him.' Pamela Hansford Johnson (page 179), on the other hand, attacks the appalling arrogance of the assumption that all women are clamouring to be loved by a man anyway. Florence Nightingale certainly wasn't. In later life, according to Lytton Strachey, she displayed strong lesbian tendencies and pounced on unfortunate little nurses who came to pay homage at her home in Smith Street. On page 174 she writes off her sex as disparagingly as any man would, for their frivolity, scattiness and total lack of interest in politics.

In two secular fourteenth-century handbooks for women, obedience to their menfolk and long-suffering compliance with their wishes are advised as religious duties. In the *Livre du Chevalier de la Tour Landry*, a manual written around 1372 by a father for his daughters, the chevalier quotes approvingly the monstrous unpleasantness of the story of Patient Griselda – whose virtue was tried by every cunning form of cruelty by her husband – and when discussing womanly obedience describes as exemplary the reaction of a wife who, when ordered by her husband, *'Sal sur la table,'* leapt on the table when he was merely asking her to pass the salt.

**Marina Warner,** ALONE OF ALL HER SEX

Now you will know that all this happened in the early days of what we called then the 'emancipation of woman'. Many strange things took place then. I do not think that at the time the movement went very deep down in the social world, but here were the young women of the highest intelligence, and the most daring and ingenious of them, coming out of the chiaroscuro of a thousand years, blinking at the sun and wild with desire to try their wings. I believe that some of them put on the armour and the halo of St Joan of Arc, who was herself an emancipated virgin, and became like white-hot angels. But most women, when they feel free to experiment with life, will go straight to the witches' Sabbath. I myself respect them for it, and do not think that I could ever really love a woman who had not, at some time or other, been up on a broomstick.

I have always thought it unfair to woman that she has never been alone in the world. Adam had a time, whether long or short, when he could wander about on a fresh and peaceful earth, among the beasts, in full possession of his soul, and most men are born with a memory of that period. But poor Eve found him there, with all his claims upon her, the moment she looked into the world. That is a grudge that woman has always had against the Creator: she feels that she is entitled to have that epoch of paradise back for herself. Only, worse luck, when chasing an epoch that has gone, one is bound to get hold of it by the tail, the wrong way round. Thus these young witches got everything they wanted as in a catoptric image.

**Isak Dinesen,** THE OLD CHEVALIER

The one thing civilization couldn't do anything about – women.

**Shelagh Delaney,** A TASTE OF HONEY

For the first time (1915) women in industry were getting breadwinners' wages . . . The projectile girls, for instance, could earn £3 4s 2d a week. It was not only five times as much as the wage they were used to, but despite war-time prices it would buy a really comfortable quantity of good food . . . A woman worker, giving evidence to an official inspector of factories, told him that she worked from 7 a.m. to 8.30 p.m. and on Sundays from 8 to 5; that she spent two hours daily travelling to and from work and was supporting an invalid husband and six children under twelve, but that she felt better than she had ever done in her life because with her wages they could all have as much as they wanted to eat every day.

**Ruth Adam,** A WOMAN'S PLACE

Women have no sympathy . . . And my experience of women is almost as large as Europe. And it is so intimate too. I have lived and slept in the same bed with English Countesses and Prussian Bauerinnen, with a closeness of intimacy no one ever had before. No Roman Catholic Supérieure has ever had charge of women of the most different creeds that I have had. No woman has excited 'passions' among women more than I have. Yet I leave no school behind me . . . Not one of my Crimean following learnt anything from me or gave herself for one moment after she came home to carry out the lessons of that war . . . No woman that I know has ever *appris à apprendre* . . . Nothing makes me so impatient as people complaining of their want of money. How can you remember what you have never heard? . . . They don't know the names of the Cabinet Ministers. They don't know the officers at the Horse Guards. They don't know who of the men of the day is dead and who is alive . . . Women crave *for being loved*, not for loving. They scream at you for sympathy all day long, they are incapable of giving *any* in return for they cannot remember your affairs long enough to do so.

**Florence Nightingale**, LETTERS TO MADAME MOHL

If I ever live and grow up my *one* aim and concentrated purpose *shall be* and *is* to show that women *can learn, can reason, can compete* with men in the grand fields of literature and science and conjecture that open before the nineteenth century, that a woman can be a woman and a *true* one without having all her time engrossed by dress and society.

**Carey Thomas**

But for Miss Garrett, I must say that I gained more from her than from any other doctor, for she not only repeated what all of the others had said, but entered much more into my mental state and way of life than they could do, because I was able to *tell* her so much more than I ever could or would to any *man.*

**Josephine Butler** on Elizabeth Garrett Anderson

The problem lay buried, unspoken for many years, in the minds of American women. It was a strange stirring, a sense of dissatisfaction . . . Each suburban wife struggled with it alone. As she made the beds, shopped for groceries, matched slipcover material, ate peanut butter sandwiches with her children, chauffeured Cub Scouts and Brownies, lay beside her husband at night – she was afraid to ask even of herself the silent question – 'Is this all?'

For over fifteen years there was no word of this yearning in the millions of words written about women, for women, in all the columns, books and articles by experts telling women their role was to seek fulfilment as wives and mothers . . . Experts told them how to catch a man and keep him, how to breastfeed children and handle their toilet training, how to cope with sibling rivalry and adolescent rebellion; how to buy a dishwasher, bake bread, cook gourmet snails and build a swimming pool with their own hands, how to dress, look, and act more feminine, and make marriage more exciting . . . They were taught to pity the neurotic, unfeminine unhappy women who wanted to be poets or physicists or presidents. They learned that truly feminine women do not want careers, higher education, political rights – the independence and the opportunities that the old-fashioned feminists fought for. Some women, in their forties and fifties, still remembered painfully giving up those dreams, but most of the younger women no longer even thought about them. A thousand expert voices applauded their femininity, their adjustment, their new maturity. All they had to do was to devote their lives from earliest girlhood to finding a husband and bearing children.

**Betty Friedan,** The Feminine Mystique

The sentimental cult of domestic virtues is the cheapest method at society's disposal of keeping women quiet without seriously considering their grievances or improving their position. It has been successfully used to this day and has helped to perpetuate some dilemmas of home-making women by telling them, on the one hand, that they are devoted to the most sacred duty, while on the other hand keeping them on a level of unpaid drudgery.

**Alva Myrdal** and **Viola Klein,** Women's Two Roles

'Women are making a blasted nuisance of themselves – forgive my language Gardenia – tying themselves to railings, screaming outside the Houses of Parliament. It makes one quite ashamed of the fair sex!'

'I personally don't want a vote,' Gardenia said, 'but I think women have a very raw deal all round. Look how they are ordered about, first by their parents, and then by their husbands. A woman never has a chance to think for herself or do anything she wants to do.'

'I will let you do anything you want to do,' Bertie said in a low voice.

'You are very kind,' Gardenia said lightly.

**Barbara Cartland,** A Virgin in Paris

The pènis is the only muscle man has that he cannot flex. It is also the only extremity he cannot control . . . But even worse, as it affects the dignity of its owner, is its seeming obedience to that inferior thing, woman. It rises at the sight, or even at the thought of a woman.

**Elizabeth Gould Davis**, THE FIRST SEX

A full bosom is actually a millstone around a woman's neck: it endears her to the men who want to make their mammet of her, but she is never allowed to think that their popping eyes actually see her . . . (Breasts) are not parts of a person but lures slung around her neck, to be kneaded and twisted like magic, putty, or mumbled and mouthed like lolly ices.

**Germaine Greer**, THE FEMALE EUNUCH

While Amy was packing up after the picnic Gareth strolled off to pick a few cowslips and have a pee. Amy went another way and squatted in a ditch, was stung on the bottom by nettles, and felt resentment at being a woman, at having to be so clumsy (she had made her shoes wet), to look so inelegant, so absurd, even though no one saw her, and to have to keep rubbing her buttocks all the afternoon because of infuriating irritation. Gareth might think her 'little trouble' had spread. Once, she had been forced to go to him with vaginal thrush. In fact, she had planned not to go to him, had chosen his day off, so that she might see his partner instead, and had then found that for some reason his day off had been changed and there he was sitting behind the desk as usual. 'He may be used to looking at horrid things like that,' she had once confessed to Martha, 'but *I* am not used to having them looked at. Especially by someone I am meeting at a party that very evening.'

**Elizabeth Taylor**, BLAMING

You who come of a younger and happier generation may not have heard of her – you may not know what I mean by The Angel in the House. I will describe her as shortly as I can. She was intensely sympathetic. She was immensely charming. She was utterly unselfish. She excelled in the difficult arts of family life. She sacrificed herself daily. If there was chicken, she took the leg; if there was a draught she sat in it – in short she was so constituted that she never had a mind or a wish of her own, but preferred to sympathize always with the minds and wishes of others. Above all – I need not say it – she was pure. Her purity was supposed to be her chief virtue – her blushes, her great grace. In those days – the last of Queen Victoria – every house had its Angel.

**Virginia Woolf**, 'PROFESSIONS FOR WOMEN',
COLLECTED ESSAYS, VOLUME II

We demand that, in that strange new world that is arising alike upon man and the woman, where nothing is as it was, and all things are assuming new shapes and relations, that in this world we also shall have our share of honoured and socially useful human toil, our full half of the labour of the Children of Woman. We demand nothing more than this, and will take nothing less. *This is our* 'WOMAN'S RIGHT'!

**Olive Schreiner,** WOMAN AND LABOUR

When I began this Militant Campaign I was a Poor Law Guardian, and it was my duty to go through a workhouse infirmary, and I shall never forget seeing a little girl of thirteen lying on a bed playing with a doll. I was told she was on the eve of becoming a mother, and she was infected with a loathsome disease, and on the point of bringing, no doubt, a diseased child into the world. Was that not enough to make me a militant Suffragette? We women suffragists have a great mission – the greatest mission the world has ever known. It is to free half the human race, and through that freedom to save the rest.

**Emmeline Pankhurst,** VOTES FOR WOMEN (1912)

There is something that Governments care for far more than human life, and that is the security of property, and so it is through property that we shall strike the enemy . . . Be militant each in your own way . . . I incite this meeting to rebellion.

**Emmeline Pankhurst,** speech in the Albert Hall, 17 October 1912

I can never feel that setting fire to houses and churches and letter-boxes and destroying valuable pictures really helps to convince people that women ought to be enfranchised.

**Dame Millicent Fawcett**

The argument of the broken pane of glass is the most valuable argument in modern politics.

**Emmeline Pankhurst,** VOTES FOR WOMEN

The Bible and Church have been the greatest stumbling blocks in the way of women's emancipation.

> Elizabeth Cady Stanton, FREE THOUGHT MAGAZINE, September 1896

I found nothing grand in the history of the Jews nor in the morals inculcated in the Pentateuch. I know of no other books that so fully teach the subjection and degradation of women.

> Elizabeth Cady Stanton, EIGHTY YEARS AND MORE

In men this blunder still you find, –
All think their little set mankind.

> Hannah More, 'FLORIO AND HIS FRIEND'

No matter how hard a man may labour, some woman is always in the background of his mind. She is the one reward of virtue.

> Gertrude Atherton, THE CONQUEROR

Blessed is the man who, having nothing to say, abstains from giving in words evidence of the fact.

> George Eliot, IMPRESSIONS OF THEOPHRASTUS SUCH

If a man is only a little lower than the angels, the angels should reform.

> Mary Wilson Little

Woman's virtue is man's greatest invention.

**Cornelia Otis Skinner**


Women are never stronger than when they arm themselves with their weakness.

**Mme du Deffand**


Women have served all these centuries as looking-glasses possessing the magic and delicious power of reflecting the figure of man at twice its natural size.

**Virginia Woolf,** A Room of One's Own


When he said we were trying to make a fool of him, I could only murmur that the Creator had beat us to it.

**Ilka Chase**


Her little kiss on his cheek was as fresh, as timid, as sweet-smelling as a child's. Touched, he realised to his surprise that she must once have been quite pretty, in a Kate Greenaway fashion. Although she had withered in loneliness on her scholarly plinth, her youth had never gone from her. It was preserved, shrunken but still perceptible, under the glass bell of age. It would be easy, he thought, to pity her: yet he doubted whether she had ever pitied herself. If she had wanted love enough, she could have had it – verve and beauty are far less compelling than the sheer desire of flesh to be taken. She had not wanted men, but she had wanted her work. She had wanted success after her own fashion. She had been perfectly happy in her way, and it was pure sentimentality to wish that her way had been otherwise. You might as well give a man a space-suit when what he wants is Proust, in two volumes, boxed.

**Pamela Hansford Johnson,** Night and Silence Who is Here?

When a man gets up to speak, people listen, then look. When a woman gets up, people *look*; then, if they like what they see, they listen.

Pauline Frederick

What is woman? Only one of nature's agreeable blunders.

**Hannah Cowley,** Who's the Dupe?

I tell you there isn't a thing under the sun that needs to be done at all, but what a man can do better than a woman, unless it's bearing children, and they do that in a poor makeshift way; it had better ha' been left to the men.

**George Eliot,** Adam Bede

A lady is smarter than a gentleman, maybe,
She can sew a fine seam, she can have a baby,
She can use her intuition instead of her brain,
But she can't fold a paper in a crowded train.

**Phyllis McGinley,** 'Trial and Error'

The great and almost only comfort about being a woman is that one can always pretend to be more stupid than one is and no one is surprised.

**Freya Stark,** The Valleys of the Assassins

A caress is better than a career.

**Elizabeth Marbury** (referring to careers for women)

'And we're all going to live happily ever afterwards,' she cried jubilantly. . . 'Oh Erica I was very much afraid you were going to grow into a superior female M.P.'

'I hope I shall never be superior or a female,' said Erica firmly. 'But I may still be an M.P. even if I do marry Derrick. It isn't impossible you know.'

'No, I suppose not,' admitted Dimsie, 'But I don't think it's advisable.'

**Dorita Fairlie Bruce,** Dimsie Grows Up

How did this notion get round that women cook only for men? Why, indeed, should we manage with some cheese just because our sexual organs are different?

**Elizabeth Taylor,** At Mrs Lippincote's

When a woman behaves like a man, why doesn't she behave like a nice man?

**Dame Edith Evans**

# Stern Array

Now we come to war. It seems ironic, after reading the last section, that two world wars did more to liberate women than all the tub-thumping of the feminists. In 1915, all the jobs of the men who went to war were taken over by women, and in 1939, as Monica Dickens points out in the opening of *One Pair of Feet*:

'It seemed that women, having been surplus for twenty years, were suddenly wanted in a hundred different places at once. You couldn't open a newspaper without being told that YOU were wanted in the Army, the Navy or the Air Force; factory wheels would stop turning unless you rushed into overalls at once, the A.F.S. could quench no fires without you, every hoarding beckoned you and even Marble Arch badgered you about the A.R.P.

'The Suffragettes could have saved themselves a lot of trouble if they had seen this coming. Men's jobs were open to women, and trousers were selling like hot cakes in Kensington High Street.'

The terrible thing about war, as Margot Asquith tells us in a rare moment of sensitivity, is that few people have much idea of the horror of it until they reach the firing line. Can dear Lady Maud Warrender really have been so insensitive to the mental torture which a man must have endured when left abandoned for several days in no-man's-land that she can honestly believe that his greatest hardship was the lack of a handkerchief? Yet this is what she appears to be saying.

We quote in this section the whole of a very fine but little known poem by Lucy Whitmell, simply because it deserves a wider audience. The last three lines admirably highlight the dislocated morality of war. The last verse also has echoes of Sir Jacob Astley's prayer before the battle of Edgehill:

'Oh Lord! Thou knowest how busy I must be this day: if I forget thee, do not thou forget me.'

Some women rather shamefacedly enjoyed the Second World War. Dorothy Sayers, for example (page 186), was delighted that war put an end to travel and dressing for dinner; but it is left to one of Angela Brazil's heroines to have the last word on self-sacrifice.

From the happy expression on their faces, you might have supposed they welcomed the War. I had met people who loved stamps, and men who loved stones and snakes – but I could not imagine any man loving war.

**Margot Asquith**

Lest Heaven be thronged with greybeards hoary,
God, who made boys for His delight,

Stoops in a day of grief and glory
  And calls them in, in from the night.
When they come trooping from the war
Our skies have many a young new star.

Katharine Tynan, 'FLOWER OF YOUTH'


We had forgotten you, or very nearly –
  You did not seem to touch us very nearly –
Of course we thought about You now and then;
Especially in any time of trouble –
We knew that You were good in time of trouble –
  But we are very ordinary men.

And there were always other things to think of –
There's a lot of things a man has got to think of –
  His work, his home, his pleasure, and his wife;
And so we only thought of You on Sunday –
Sometimes, perhaps, not even on a Sunday –
  Because there's always lots to fill one's life.

And, all the while, in street or lane or byway –
In country lane, in city street, or byway –
  You walked among us, and we did not see.
Your feet were bleeding as You walked our pavements –
How *did* we miss Your footprints on our pavements? –
  Can there be other folk as blind as we?

*Now* we remember; over here in Flanders –
(It isn't strange to think of You in Flanders) –
  This hideous warfare seems to make things clear.
We never thought about You much in England –
But now that we are far away from England,
  We have no doubts, we know that You are here.

You helped us pass the jest along the trenches –
Where, in cold blood, we waited in the trenches –
  You touched its ribaldry and made it fine.
You stood beside us in our pain and weakness –
We're glad to think You understand our weakness –
  Somehow it seems to help us not to whine.

We think about You kneeling in the Garden –
Ah! God! the agony of that dread Garden –
  We know You prayed for us upon the cross.
If anything could make us glad to bear it –
'Twould be the knowledge that You willed to bear it –
  Pain – death – the uttermost of human loss.

Though we forgot You – You will not forget us –
We feel so sure that You will not forget us –
   But stay with us until this dream is past.
And so we ask for courage, strength and pardon –
Especially, I think, we ask for pardon –
   And that You'll stand beside us to the last.

> **Lucy Whitmell**, 'CHRIST IN FLANDERS' (first published
> in The SPECTATOR on 11 September 1915)

Keep the home fires burning,
While your hearts are yearning,
Though your lads are far away
They dream of home.
There's a silver lining
Through the dark clouds shining,
Turn the dark clouds inside out
Till the boys come home.

> **Lena Guilbert Ford**, 'KEEP THE HOME FIRES
> BURNING'

She (Lady Blanche Gordon-Lennox) also told me that one of the most
painful things she had seen was an officer who had been left out in No-
Man's-Land for several days. Not only badly wounded, but suffering
from a terrible cold in the head, but minus a handkerchief, with only
the sleeve of his coat to help matters, with the result that his poor face
was in a ghastly condition when he arrived at Boulogne.

> **Lady Maud Warrender**, MY FIRST 60 YEARS

That day Mr Steed brought down with him a copy of *The Journal*. In it
was a picture of a woman and her little boy standing beside one of the
many battle crosses that were the only crop I saw in the north of France
after the war, and the little boy is saying: *'Mère, est-ce que père sait que
nous sommes vainqueurs?'* The paper was lying on a side-table and I
called the Empress's attention to the picture, reading aloud the text,
which I knew her dim eyes could not decipher. I shall never forget how
she gripped my arm in her amazingly strong fingers, and, looking
across the park towards the Mausoleum, whispered: *'Je l'ai bien dit aux
miens la-bas!'*

> **Dame Ethel Smyth**, STREAKS OF LIFE*

---

*During the First World War the Empress Eugénie, widow of Napoleon III, turned her house in Surrey into a military hospital. The soldiers who died were buried in the park.

To hear Alice talk about her escape from France, one would have thought that she had swum the Channel with her maid between her teeth.

Mrs Greville on Mrs Keppel in 1939

To make ideas effective, we must be able to fire them off. We must put them into action . . . 'I will not cease from mental fight,' Blake wrote. Mental fight means thinking against the current, not with it. The current flows fast and furious. It issues in a spate of words from the loudspeakers and the politicians. Every day they tell us that we are a free people fighting to defend freedom. That is the current that has whirled the young airman up into the sky and keeps him circulating there among the clouds. Down here, with a roof to cover us and a gasmask handy, it is our business to puncture gasbags and discover the seeds of truth.

Virginia Woolf, NEW REPUBLIC, 21 OCTOBER 1940

His (her son, Charles) only complaint was that their conversation, with the words 'bloody' or 'fucking' occurring in every sentence, got badly on his nerves. Yet a remark using only one of these words, which I heard a soldier say in a canteen in the four years' war, didn't shock me or any who heard him. It was as if he were saying 'It's the idling, loafing about, not the fighting, that gets on your nerves'. What he said, seriously, with no desire to shock, so that no one *was* shocked, was: 'It isn't the fucking fighting that fucks us, its the fucking fucking about.'

Christabel Aberconway, A WISER WOMAN?

I'm glad we've been bombed. It makes me feel I can look the East End in the face.

Queen Elizabeth (now the Queen Mother) after the bombing of Buckingham Palace in 1940

From "Lord, I Thank Thee—" by Dorothy L. Sayers

IF IT were not for the war,
This war
Would suit me down to the ground. . . .

I have always detested travelling
And now there is no travelling to do. . . .

I need not buy new clothes,
Or change for dinner,

Or bother to make up my face—
It is virtuous to refrain from these things.
I need not shiver in silk stockings;—
I had a hunch about wool before it was rationed;
Now I have knitted myself woollen stocking
That come a long way up. . . .

As it happens, I like knitting
And nothing gratifies one more
Than to be admired for doing what one likes. . . .

I am better off with vegetables
At the bottom of my garden
Than with all the fairies of the 'Midsummer Night's Dream'

Dorothy L. Sayers, 'LONDON CALLING: LORD, I
THANK THEE'

What would Mother do when this war was over and the canteen was closed and she was left with but one son (if that, indeed) instead of those dozens of 'my boys', towards all of whom she felt like a mother? A retired colonel, however fire-eating, takes up gardening or plays golf or bridge or busies himself with local administration or rings migratory birds, for men are flippant, variable, easily amused. But to a woman's iron energies what appeasement can peace bring?

Sylvia Townsend Warner, ENGLISH CLIMATE

'Just as you like,' said Mr Dexter. 'Then I call on Charlie. There is one thing we here in Europe are very anxious to know, Charlie, and that is what, if any, air-raid precautions are being taken in New York?'
        'Well, Heck, quite some precautions are being taken. In the first place the authorities have issued a very comprehensive little pamphlet entitled "The Bomb and You" designed to bring the bomb into every home and invest it with a certain degree of cosiness. This should calm and reassure the population in case of attack. There are plenty of guidance reunions, fork lunches, and so on where the subject is treated frankly, to familiarize it, as it were, and rob it of all unpleasantness.'

Nancy Mitford, THE BLESSING

It is the duty of every British girl to make every possible sacrifice to keep those unspeakable Huns out of our islands. I appeal to you all to use the utmost economy and abstinence, and voluntarily to give up some of the things that you like . . .
        'It'll mean knocking off buns, I suppose,' sighed Sylvia mournfully.

Angela Brazil, A PATRIOTIC SCHOOLGIRL

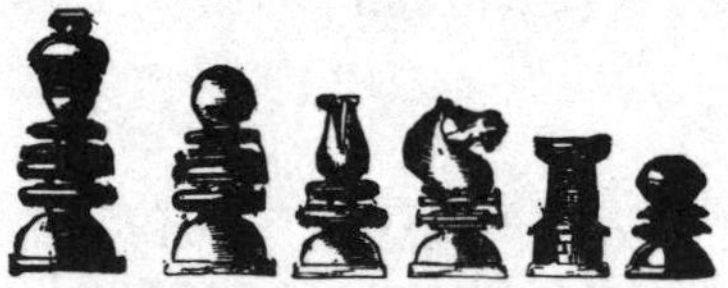

# Crown and State

England has, in the past, always thrived under a woman's rule. This, according to a French Duchess (page 190) is because rulers always listen to their advisers, and women are always advised by men. One of the exceptions was Queen Anne, who for a long time was under the spell of the beautiful but choleric and overbearing Sarah Churchill. From Sarah's letter, quoted on this page, one would think that during her reign as favourite she was a model of sweetness and subservience. History books and contemporary reports, however, tell us a different story; Sarah bullied the Queen unmercifully. Once again, to quote Edith Sitwell, 'There is no truth, there are only points of view.'

As an example of *noblesse oblige,* we have poor Queen Victoria, distraught with grief after the death of Albert, having to expose herself to the curious stares of her subjects when she opens Parliament. One pities her so much that one is slightly reluctant to accept Muriel Spark's screamingly funny and thoroughly iconoclastic explanation as to why Victoria was considered responsible for the rise of democracy in the British Isles. Anyway, it is a relief to see that the Queen had cheered up enough twelve years later, on the anniversary of Albert's birthday, to give her faithful John Brown some nice presents (page 191).

Our own royal family are not famed for their witty repartee. A friend who worked for one of the great London couturiers remembered the present Queen admiring a very glamorous hat. When it was suggested she might like it, she merely smiled and replied: 'Oh no, we already have a hat.' On page 192 we find her in a less genial mood putting her sister's children firmly in their place.

Those of high rank usually feel it their duty to keep in touch with the lower echelons. The Queen Mother achieved this by listening to Mrs Dale. She, it must be acknowledged, is certainly able to find the apt remark at the right moment. Once when visiting an art gallery and finding herself expected to comment upon a picture which consisted of six square feet of canvas covered with black paint, relieved only by a small strip of green in one corner, she turned to the artist and said: 'I always think a little green does so help a picture, don't you?'

We then move on to politics, leaving it to the Prime Minister to have the last word. It is, after all, a woman's privilege to change her mind.

If it were in my power, I would not be a favourite, which few will believe . . . as fond as people are of power, I fancy that anybody that had been shut up so many tedious hours as I have been with a person that had no conversation, and yet must be treated with respect, would feel something of what I did, and be very glad, when their circumstances did not want it, to be freed from such slavery, which must be uneasy at all times, though I do protest that upon the account of her loving me and trusting me so entirely as she did, I had a concern for her which was more than you will easily believe, and I would have served her with the hazard of my life upon any occasion; but after she put me at liberty by using me ill, I was very easy, and liked better that anybody should have her favour than myself at the price of flattery, without which I believe nobody can be well with a King or a Queen.

> **Sarah Churchill, Duchess of Marlborough,** LETTER,
> 23 APRIL 1711

Kings show their pity in doing justice, and do justice in showing pity.

> **cinska**

The sovereign is absolute; for, in a state whose expanse is so vast, there can be no other appropriate authority except that which is concentrated in him . . . It is better to obey the laws of one master than to seek to please several . . . The intention of autocracy is the glory of the citizen, the state and the sovereign.

> **Catherine the Great**

During his visit to Russia Diderot remarked upon the uncleanliness of the peasants. 'Why', replied the Empress Catherine II 'should they take care of a body that does not belong to them?' *(Pourquoi auraient-ils soin d'un corps que ne leur appartient pas?)*

The Duchess of Burgundy asked Louis XIV why in England Queens governed better than Kings. She answered her own question thus: 'Because under Kings it is the women who govern, and men under Queens.'*

---

*Barbara Wilson tells the same story in *The House of Memories* but substitutes Mme de Maintenon for Louis XIV.

The Queen *must say* that she does feel *very bitterly* the want of feeling of those who *ask* the Queen to go to open Parliament. That the public should wish to see her she fully understands, and has no wish to prevent – quite the contrary; but why this wish should be of so *unreasonable* and unfeeling a nature, as to *long* to witness the spectacle of a poor broken-hearted widow, nervous and shrinking, dragged in *deep mourning*, ALONE *in* STATE as a show, where she used to go supported by her husband, to be gazed at, without delicacy of feeling, is a thing she cannot understand, and she could never wish her bitterest foe to be exposed to!

**Queen Victoria** to Earl Russell, 1866

The real rise of democracy in the British Isles occurred in Scotland by means of Queen Victoria's bladder . . . When she went to stay at Balmoral in her latter years a number of privies were caused to be built at the backs of little cottages which had not previously possessed privies. This was to enable the Queen to go on her morning drive round the countryside in comfort, and to descend from her carriage from time to time, ostensibly to visit the humble cottagers in their dwellings. Eventually, word went round that Queen Victoria was exceedingly democratic. Of course it was all due to her little weakness. But everyone copied the Queen and the idea spread, and now you see we have a great democracy.

**Muriel Spark,** MEMENTO MORI

Again this dear and blessed anniversary returns, and again without my beloved blessed One! But he is ever with me in spirit.

When I came down to breakfast, I gave Beatrice a mounted photograph of our dear Mausoleum, and a silver belt of Montenegrin workmanship. After breakfast I gave my faithful Brown an oxidised silver biscuit-box, and some onyx studs. He was greatly pleased with the former, and tears came into his eyes, and he said: 'It is too much.' God knows, it is not for one so devoted and faithful.

**Queen Victoria,** JOURNAL OF OUR LIFE IN THE HIGHLANDS, 26 August 1878

The occasion I am speaking of, when I first came into contact with her (the Empress Eugénie), was a meet of the harriers, which took place, at her special request, at Farnborough Hill. She came out onto the gravel sweep in front of the house, and her manner was more gracious and winning than any manner I had ever seen as she bowed right and left to the awestruck field, saying repeatedly, 'Put on your 'ats; I pray you, put on your 'ats.' The Master was then presented, and she really and truly did remark to him – as, if you come to think of it, she naturally would – 'I 'ope the 'ounds will find the 'are near the 'ouse.'

**Dame Ethel Smyth,** Streaks of Life

Oh indeed I should cried Mr Salteena I am very fond of fresh air and royalties.

**Daisy Ashford,** The Young Visiters

Lady Montdore loved anybody royal. It was a genuine emotion, quite disinterested, since she loved them as much in exile as in power, and the act of curtsying was the consummation of this love. Her curtsies, owing to the solid quality of her frame, did not recall the graceful movement of wheat before the wind. She scrambled down like a camel, rising again backside foremost like a cow, a strange performance, painful it might be supposed to the performer, the expression on whose face, however, belied this thought. Her knees cracked like revolver shots but her smile was heavenly.

**Nancy Mitford,** Love in a Cold Climate

He was born to be a salesman. He would be an admirable representative of Rolls-Royce. But an ex-King cannot start selling motor-cars.

**Duchess of Windsor** in Harold Nicolson's Diary
28 May 1947

They are not royal. They just happen to have me as their aunt.

**H.M. the Queen** about Princess Margaret's children, Daily Mail, 4 October 1977

My favourite programme is *Mrs Dale's Diary*. I try never to miss it because it is the only way of knowing what goes on in a middle-class family.

### Queen Elizabeth, the Queen Mother

I was born in the 'eighties into a sheltered, comfortable, religious and literary circle.

Politics to this *milieu* seemed harmless and diverting matters for academic dispute. Politicians were then noble gentlemen unpaid, and a Conservative was then a Conservative and a Liberal a Liberal. The earliest election I can remember seemed to be a game with an old gentleman called Lord Salisbury climbing up a ladder every morning in *The Times,* neck and neck with an old gentleman called Mr Gladstone on another ladder, who finally reached the top rung first.

### Mary MacCarthy, A NINETEENTH CENTURY CHILDHOOD

I saw Mr Gladstone in the street last night. I waited and waited but no cab ran him over.

### Eliza Savage

There was one bath in the whole house, and that was in my father's bedroom . . . and there was not a single bookshelf except that containing Hansard in the hall. Therefore, I asked myself, has no Prime Minister in the past ever washed or read?

### Lady Violet Bonham Carter – in a description of Number 10 given to Norman St John Stevas MP and published in THE TIMES SATURDAY REVIEW, 15 November 1969

'Ladies an' gentlemen,' said Douglas, 'I'm makin' this speech to ask you all to be Lib'rals same as what I am . . . My aunt's gotter parrot that talks, an' I'll let you come an' listen to it through the window when she's not there if you'll vote Lib'rals . . . I'll let you look at my rabbits too, an' I'll give you all a suck of rock if my aunt sends me a stick when she goes to Brighton same as she did last year.' He sat down breathless. There were certainly the makings of a politician in Douglas. He didn't care what he promised.

**Richmal Crompton,** WILLIAM THE BAD

My son was going to the Junior Branch of the Cathedral School and his friend was Elliot, Franklin Roosevelt's son. Elliot had been behaving badly and was spending the Easter Holidays locked in his bedroom.

'Poor Elliot' said all the other little boys – and felt a bit superior to him. But lo and behold, one morning a Communist was walking by Elliot's window when a bomb was thrown at him and blew the Communist up. Through Elliot's window came one of the Communist's legs and landed on the scrambled eggs Elliot was eating.

All the newspapers made great stories of this. Pictures of Elliot and the leg were front-page news, and Elliot overnight became famous. 'Just Elliot's luck!' said the other boys wistfully.

**Molly Berkeley,** BEADED BUBBLES

During the last few weeks I have felt that the Suez Canal was flowing through my drawing room.

**Lady Eden** (at the time of the Suez Canal crisis, 1956)

He is used to dealing with estate workers. I cannot see how anyone can say he is out of touch.

**Lady Caroline Douglas-Home** (when her father
became Prime Minister), DAILY HERALD,
21 October 1963

No woman in my time will be Prime Minister or Chancellor or Foreign Secretary – not the top jobs. Anyway I wouldn't want to be Prime Minister. You have to give yourself 100%.

**Mrs Thatcher,** interview in the SUNDAY TELEGRAPH on 26 October 1969, on her appointment as Shadow Education Spokesman

# Ordered Abroad

'I loathe abroad, nothing would induce me to live there, I'd rather live in the gamekeeper's hut in Hensgrove and as for foreigners, they are all the same, they make me sick.' Such rampant xenophobia could only come from Nancy Mitford's Uncle Matthew. But one suspects that a lot of women subconsciously agree with him, not so much because they loathe abroad but because they detest the hassle of getting there – all the palaver of holiday wardrobes, of putting dogs in kennels, of finding someone to water the plants and feed the cats, and, if you're taking the children, of filling five extra suitcases with baby food and collapsible nappies. Many women, as was pointed out in the section on houses and gardens, hate leaving home. But the desire to put down roots is so strong that, having got abroad and settled in only for a few days, they feel uprooted when they have to come home again. Anne Lindbergh sums up this feeling perfectly on this page.

Fanny Burney, on the other hand, found abroad so visually seductive that she couldn't bear to look at England on her return, and Edna St Vincent Millay (page 198), although she swears to remain faithful to her lover if she stays at home, says she won't be responsible for her actions if she ever travels. Very much like the male principle of a broad being allowed if it's abroad.

The Irish are notoriously difficult to write about; if you are nice about them they accuse you of being patronising; if you attack them you're just behaving in a typically brutal English fashion. On page 201 Edna O'Brien puts into words what one has always suspected, that the Irish can be very funny and sharp, but are too paranoid and bedevilled by their dark history to take jokes against themselves.

That familiar indefinable lump in the chest . . . the going-away lump, that had been there when I was a child and was as uncontrollable now as then. Leaving the seaside after the summer was over; leaving home for the seaside; leaving houses, country and city, casual and important, temporary and permanent – any place that you had made with difficulty and affection your home. In fact, simply going away.

**Anne Morrow Lindbergh**, LISTEN, THE WIND

Once when Beerbohm Tree came home from a holiday in Paris she (Lady Tree) asked him if he had enjoyed himself. 'Oh yes, I did, but

Paris was thronged with hundreds of appalling Cook's tourists.' 'Ah,' she said, 'I suppose too many Cooks spoiled the brothels!'

Lady Maud Warrender, My First 60 Years

I feel about airplanes the way I feel about diets. It seems to me that they are wonderful things for other people to go on.

Jean Kerr, The Snake Has All the Lines

I always say that a girl never really looks as well as she does on board a steamship, or even a yacht.

Anita Loos, Gentlemen Prefer Blondes

The fabric of my faithful love
   No power shall dim or ravel
Whilst I stay here – but oh, my dear,
   If I should ever travel!

Edna St Vincent Millay, 'To The Not Impossible Him'

The English have always been a wicked race, but since their King William they have become worse and fallen into very vicious ways. It has been noticed that islanders are always more treacherous and wicked than the inhabitants of terra firma.

Charlotte Elizabeth ('Liselotte'), Duchess of Orleans,<br/>in a letter to her stepmother Louisa, 13 January 1718

They make other nations seem pale and flighty,
But they do think England is God almighty,
And you must remind them now and then
That other countries breed other men.

**Alice Duer Miller,** 'The White Cliffs'

Americans, indeed, often seem to be so overwhelmed by their children that they'll do anything for them except stay married to the co-producer.

**Katharine Whitehorn,** Observations

This Englishwoman is so refined
She has no bosom and no behind.

**Stevie Smith,** 'This Englishwoman'

Gertrude Stein used to get furious when the english all talked about german organisation. She used to insist that the germans had no organisation, they had method but no organisation. Don't you understand the difference, she used to say angrily, any two americans any twenty americans, any millions of americans can organise themselves to do something but germans cannot organise themselves to do anything, they can formulate a method and this method can be put upon them but this isn't organisation. The germans, she used to insist, are not modern, they are a backward people who have made a method of what we conceive as organisation, can't you see. They cannot therefore possibly win this war because they are not modern.

**Gertrude Stein,** The Autobiography of
Alice B. Toklas*

---

* 'Gertrude Stein and me are just like brothers.'
  Ernest Hemingway, quoted in John
Malcolm Brinnin, *The Third Rose.*

In the United States there is more space where nobody is than where anybody is.

That is what makes America what it is.

Gertrude Stein, THE GEOGRAPHICAL HISTORY OF AMERICA

Travelling is the ruin of all happiness! There's no looking at a building here after seeing Italy.

Fanny Burney, CECILIA

Europeans used to say Americans were puritanical. Then they discovered that we were not puritans. So now they say we are obsessed with sex.

Mary McCarthy, LADY WITH A SUITABLE LIFE

The Jews are among the aristocracy of every land; if a literature is called rich in the possession of a few classic tragedies, what shall we say to a national tragedy lasting fifteen hundred years in which the poets and actors were also the heroes?

George Eliot, DANIEL DERONDA

How is progress doing in Africa? Oh good. One hardly dares to ask that question, for I so rarely like the answer. Progress everywhere today does seem to come so very heavily disguised as Chaos.

Joyce Grenfell, STATELY AS A GALLEON

When a white man in Africa by accident looks into the eyes of a native and sees the human being (which it is his chief preoccupation to avoid), his sense of guilt, which he denies, fumes up in resentment and he brings down the whip.

**Doris Lessing,** THE GRASS IS SINGING

Mr Dickinson declares that some of the young English gentlemen in Geneva have angered the Genevois, who are excessively prudish, by their follies and excesses. Apropos of Mrs Templeton, her absurd French is the laugh of the town. The other evening at a party she was exclaiming on the cold of this country, and how she was constrained to sleep between two mattresses for warmth, but as she committed the amazing error of saying *'Il faut que je me couche entre deux matelots',* the entire company was thrown into fits of merriment.

**Cleonie Knox,** THE DIARY OF A YOUNG LADY OF FASHION IN THE YEAR 1764–5

When anyone asks me about the Irish character, I say look at the trees. Maimed, stark and misshapen, but ferociously tenacious. The Irish have got gab but are too touchy to be humorous. Me too.

**Edna O'Brien**

The Englishman fox-trots as he fox-hunts, with all his being, through thickets, through ditches, over hedges, through chiffons, through waiters, over saxophones, to the victorious finish: and who goes home depends on how many the ambulance will accommodate.

**Edna St Vincent Millay**

# Time's Malicious Dart

'Age wins, and one must learn to grow old,' wrote Lady Diana Cooper, and, as both Edna Ferber and Emerald Cunard point out, growing old is much easier when you give up the struggle against it.

There is something rather restful about the marriage of Elizabeth Jennings's parents (page 205), when all passion is spent. One does rather wonder, however, if Miss Jennings's parents ever read the poem. Children are always inclined to underestimate their parents' sexuality, preferring to regard their mother as the Virgin Mary, and to believe that they themselves were born by internal combustion.

Few people, even when they reach advanced age, are immune from romance. Sylvia Townsend Warner beautifully describes the elderly spinster who always reads biographies, but who switches from the well regulated lives of bishops and generals to the more romantic ones of opera singers and royal favourites at the beginning of autumn to cheer herself up.

On page 205 we have Dame Ethel Smitten again, drooling this time over a certain Madame de Bülow, and stating truthfully that women who've been very much loved retain even in old age the ability to dazzle. In fact, if you examine the effect of the great spellbinders you will find that they enchant as much by their wit and charm as their looks. One of the great flaws in Helen of Troy's character was that she never made any jokes. Who, for example, could resist Lady Diana Cooper in her eighties telling a man from the pensions office who asked her age that he could look it up in *Burke's Peerage*. Or Dame Rebecca West, who, having invited a handsome American publisher to dine at her flat and talked long into the night, asked him as he got up to go if he'd mind unzipping her dress at the back.

'It would be a pleasure,' he said.

'No,' she replied, her eyes twinkling, 'at my age it's not a pleasure, it's a privilege.'


The years that a woman subtracts from her age are not lost. They are added to the ages of other women.

**Diane de Poitiers**


The post-office has a great charm at one period of our lives. When you have lived to my age, you will begin to think letters are never worth going through the rain for.

**Jane Austen, EMMA**

A woman's always younger than a man
At equal years.

> Elizabeth Barrett Browning, 'AURORA LEIGH'

It's no trifle at her time of life to part with a doctor who knows her constitution.

> George Eliot, JANET'S REPENTANCE

The years seem to rush by now, and I think of death as a fast approaching end of a journey – double and treble reasons for loving as well as working while it is day.

> George Eliot, LIFE AND LETTERS

All one's life as a young woman one is on show, a focus of attention, people notice you. You set yourself up to be noticed and admired. And then, not expecting it, you become middle-aged and anonymous. No one notices you. You achieve a wonderful freedom. It is a positive thing. You can move about, unnoticed and invisible.

> Doris Lessing

I shall never get used to not being the most beautiful woman in the room. It was an intoxication to sweep in and know every man had turned his head. It kept me in form.

> Lady Randolph Churchill, quoted in Anita Leslie's JENNIE

Lying apart now, each in a separate bed,
He with a book, keeping the light on late,
She like a girl dreaming of childhood,
All men elsewhere – it is as if they wait
Some new event: the book he holds unread,
Her eyes fixed on the shadows overhead.

Tossed up like a flotsam from a former passion,
How cool they lie. They hardly ever touch,
Or if they do it is like a confession
Of having little feeling – or too much
Chastity faces them, a destination
For which their whole lives were a preparation.

Strangely apart, yet strangely close together,
Silence between them like a thread to hold
And not wind in. And time itself's a feather
Touching them gently. Do they know they're old,
These two who are my father and my mother
Whose fire from which I came, has now grown cold?

**Elizabeth Jennings**, 'ONE FLESH'

Another English exile in New York was Somerset Maugham, whom
Emerald had known ever since her marriage to Sir Bache. She had
always enjoyed sparring with him in conversation, though he did not
relish verbal duels with her on the telephone in the small hours of the
morning, since he believed in early nights as a means of remaining
young. Once, after dining with her, he prepared to leave at his usual
early hour. 'But you can't go now,' she objected, 'the evening has only
just begun!'

'I dare say, Emerald, but I have to keep my youth.'

'Then why didn't you bring him with you?' she asked. 'I should
be delighted to meet him.'

**Daphne Fielding**, EMERALD AND NANCY

She was now over 50 and had been very handsome in her youth, and
though nowadays she was only handsome occasionally, it was easy to
credit all one had heard about the passions she had inspired . . . and in
one or two cases reciprocated. People who have been much loved retain

even in old age a radiating quality difficult to describe but unmistakable. Even a stone that has been blazed on all day by a southern sun will hold heat long after nightfall; and Madame de Bülow, who was far from being a stone and not yet at the close of her day, had this warm radiance.

**Dame Ethel Smyth,** STREAKS OF LIFE

Being an old maid is like death by drowning, a really delightful sensation after you cease to struggle.

**Edna Ferber**

Before we came away, I bought a special cream supposed to restore elasticity to the skin, but I destroyed the wrapper on the jar and the accompanying, incriminating literature, as furtively as I had, when young, removed the cover of a book on sex.

**Nina Bawden,** A WOMAN OF MY AGE

Since 1936 Miss St John had lived at the Peacock Hotel, occupying bedroom number five on the second floor and, between 8.30 and 8.50 a.m., the second-floor bathroom, eating breakfast, lunch, tea and dinner, going to the Abbey Church on Sundays, the cinema on Tuesdays and Fridays, and the public library whenever she wanted another biography. The biographies she preferred were those of diplomats, sovereigns, bishops, generals, royal academicians and approved educationalists. Herself leading a regular life, she liked to read of regular lives – lives of well-conducted prosperity closing in well-attended funerals. In autumn, however, when swallows migrate to Africa and the more delicate public shrubs are wrapped in sacking, she allowed herself to read the lives of opera singers and royal favourites. Such a change was in keeping with the seasonal change from cress sandwiches to buttered crumpets.

**Sylvia Townsend Warner,** UNDER NEW MANAGEMENT

There's not much to say. I haven't been at all deedy.

**Ivy Compton-Burnett** (when asked about her life),
THE TIMES, 30 August 1969

When I was young I was frightened I might bore other people, now I'm old I am frightened they will bore me.

**Ruth Adam**

She parried time's malicious dart
And kept the years at bay
Till passion entered in her heart
And aged her in a day.

**Ella Wheeler Wilcox**

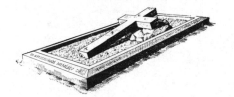

# The Happy Dead

In the nineteenth century everyone accepted and talked naturally about death. Indeed, with the rate of infant mortality what it was, it would have been impossible for a child to be shielded from the reality of death. Sex was the great taboo then, with babies being discovered under gooseberry bushes and the Count in Lampedusa's book *The Leopard* complaining that his wife had borne him umpteen children but he had never seen her navel.

Today everyone talks about sex and birth quite naturally. It is death that has become taboo. Perhaps it is because most of us no longer believe implicitly in an afterlife that we cannot face up to the terror of death and therefore sweep everything under the carpet. Consequently nineteenth-century writers treat the subject of death much more straightforwardly, while modern writers usually resort to irony, laughing to stop themselves crying.

We kick off with that dynamic duo, Ann and Jane Taylor, who were last seen exhorting Sunday-school children to greater goodness, now reminding the wicked they are destined for hell, contrasted, for good measure, with Mrs Alexander striking a more cheerful note on the same theme. One has always had one's doubts about the respective merits of heaven and hell; Katharine Whitehorn once wrote: 'In heaven they will bore you, in hell you will bore them.' Harriet Martineau, however, whose avowed atheism shocked the nineteenth century, points out (page 213) that anyone who experienced five minutes of hell would infinitely prefer being snuffed out like a candle.

Extinction too would be preferable to the poor man in the Stevie Smith poem (page 213) who, having been bullied by his relations and henpecked by his wife all his life, suddenly learns there will be no escape from them in an afterlife. I always wanted to know what happened to the Wife of Bath when she reached the other side and found her four husbands waiting for her.

From the nineteenth century we particularly liked Christina Rossetti's poem (page 212) about the incongruity of a loved one's death in the spring, when everything is budding and burgeoning, and putting out new life around you.

The death of the man she loved, who was killed in the American Civil War, inspired Elizabeth Phelps, a young American girl, to write one of the great best-sellers of the nineteenth century. We choose an extract in which the author is passionately inveighing against the social mores of the day, which expected a newly bereaved person to endure calls of sympathy from all and sundry. This outcry against exposing one's private grief to the masses has echoes of Queen Victoria's letter to Lord Russell on page 191.

We have also quoted a passage from Edith Wharton (page 215) about the inevitability of fate. This must be one of the most chilling stories of all times. It appears in a different version in John O'Hara's novel *Appointment in Samarra,* where the story had been somewhat cleaned up.

It is incredible that Wordsworth should have so admired Anna Barbauld's poem on page 212 that he wished he had written it himself. One suspects William was totally lacking in critical faculty. On the one hand he can open a poem with:

Jones! As from Calais Southward you and I
Went pacing side by side.

and then can produce lines as succinct and exquisite as:

Suffering is permanent, obscure and dark
And shares the nature of infinity.

This same idea of the infinite nature of suffering is touched upon by Emily Dickinson in her poem: 'Because I could not stop for death'. (page 211). She sees death as a courtly Southern gentleman who offers her a lift in his carriage, and is so polite as they ride along that she hardly notices that all the symbols of life – children playing, cornfields in the sun – are being left behind. Only the moment when she suddenly becomes aware that she is dying is so terrible that it seems to go on for ever.

We end with Stevie Smith's saddest and most famous lines. But, as Ivy Compton-Burnett once pointed out, 'A little black does help to add a touch of colour to the greyness of life.'

So, while their bodies moulder here
    Their souls with God himself shall dwell, –
But always recollect, my dear,
    That wicked people go to hell.

**Ann** and **Jane Taylor**, 'About Dying'

Goldsmith tells us that when lovely woman stoops to folly, she has nothing to do but to die; and when she stoops to be disagreeable, it is equally to be recommended as a clearer of ill-fame. Mrs Churchill, after being disliked at least twenty-five years, was now spoken of with compassionate allowances. In one point she was fully justified. She had never been admitted before to be seriously ill. The event acquitted her of all the fancifulness, and all the selfishness of imaginary complaints.

**Jane Austen**, Emma

So when the friends we love the best
  Lie in their churchyard bed,
We must not cry too bitterly
  Over the happy dead.

**Mrs Alexander,** 'WITHIN THE CHURCHYARD'

We all have a chance of meeting with some pity, some tenderness, some charity, when we are dead; it is the living only who cannot be forgiven.

**George Eliot,** THE LIFTED VEIL

There are only two trifles which make his funeral ovation difficult – the life and death of the subject of it.

**Mme de Sévigné,** at the death of Mgr de Harlay, the worldly Archbishop of Paris

Because I could not stop for Death –
He kindly stopped for me –
The Carriage held but just Ourselves –
And Immortality.

We slowly drove – He knew no haste
And I had put away
My labor and my leisure too,
For His Civility –

We passed the School, where Children strove
At Recess – in the Ring –
We passed the Fields of Gazing Grain –
We passed the Setting Sun
. . .
Since then – 'tis Centuries – and yet
Feels shorter than the Day
I first surmised the Horses' Heads
Were toward Eternity –

**Emily Dickinson,** 'BECAUSE I COULD NOT STOP FOR DEATH'

Why were you born when the snow was falling?
You should have come to the cuckoo's calling,
Or when grapes are green in the cluster,
Or at least when lithe swallows muster
    For their far off flying
    From summer dying.

Why did you die when the lambs were cropping?
You should have died at the apple's dropping,
When the grasshoppers come to trouble,
And the wheatfields are sodden stubble
    And all the winds go sighing
    For sweet things dying.

Christina Rossetti, 'A Dirge'

Life! we've been long together,
Through pleasant and through cloudy weather;
'Tis hard to part when friends are dear,
Perhaps 'twill cost a sigh, a tear;
Then steal away, give little warning;
Choose thine own time;
Say not 'Good-night'; but in some brighter clime
Bid me 'Good-morning'.

Anna Letitia Barbauld, 'Ode to Life'*

Never does one feel oneself so utterly helpless as in trying to speak comfort for great bereavement. I will not try it. Time is the only comforter for the loss of a mother.

Jane Carlyle

*It is surprising to learn that Wordsworth said of this stanza: 'I am not in the habit of grudging people their good things but I wish I had written these lines.'

I cannot think of any future as at all probable, except the 'annihilation' from which some people recoil with so much horror. I find myself here in the universe, – I know not how, whence, or why. I see everything in the universe go out and disappear, and I see no reason for supposing that it is not an actual and entire death. And for my part, I have no objection to such an extinction. I well remember the passion with which W. E. Forster said to me, 'I had rather be damned than annihilated.' If he once felt five minutes' damnation, he would be thankful for extinction in preference. The truth is, I care little about it anyway.

**Harriet Martineau,** in a letter to Henry Atkinson*

You've heard it before but in case you forgot death isn't a
    passing away
It's just a carrying on with friends relations and brightness
Only you don't have to bother with sickness and there's no
    financial tightness.
Mrs Simpkins went home and told her husband he was a weak-
    pated fellow
And when he heard the news he turned a daffodil shade of
    yellow
'What do you mean, Maria?' he cried, 'it can't be true there's no rest
From one's uncles and brothers and sisters nor even the wife
    of one's breast?'

**Stevie Smith,** 'MRS SIMPKINS'

All quiet along the Potomac tonight,
    No sound save the rush of the river,
While soft falls the dew on the face of the dead –
    The picket's off duty for ever.

**Ethel Lynn Beers,** 'All Quiet Along the Potomac'

---

*I fancied you would be struck by Miss Martineau's lucid and able style. She is a very admirable woman - and the most logical intellect of the age, for a woman. On this account it is that the men throw stones at her, and that many of her own sex throw dirt; but if I begin of this subject I shall end by gnashing my teeth.

**Elizabeth Barrett Browning,** letter to H. S. Boyd, 24 December 1844

Who originated that most exquisite of inquisitions, the condolence system? . . . I know that there are those who like these calls; but why, in the name of all sweet pity, must we endure them without respect of persons, as we would endure a wedding reception or make a party call? . . . I am sure I do not mean to be ungrateful for real sorrowful sympathy, however imperfectly it may be shown, or that near friends (if one has them) cannot give, in such a time as this, actual strength, even if they fail to comfort, by look, and tone, and love. But it is not near friends who are apt to wound, nor real sympathy which sharpens the worst of needles. It is the fact that all your chance acquaintances feel called upon to bring their curious eyes and jarring words right into the silence of your first astonishment; taking you in a round of morning calls with kid gloves and parasol, and the liberty to turn your heart about and cut into it at pleasure. You may quiver at every touch, but there is no escape, because it is 'the thing'.

Elizabeth Stuart Phelps, THE GATES AJAR*

Whenever I prepare for a journey I prepare as though for death. Should I never return, all is in order. This is what life has taught me.

Katherine Mansfield, JOURNAL**

---

*Crashing into all normal life, destroying its balance and its beauty, came the Civil War; and to her (Elizabeth Phelps) it brought a personal tragedy. The shock caused by the death of the boy whom she loved proved almost too much to her physical and mental poise, and for several years she was very nearly a recluse. From the grief of that period and the long brooding emerged The Gates Ajar, begun in 1864 and published in 1868 . . . . The result was amazing to the author, as, for different reasons, it is to readers today. In a tale almost devoid of incident, by means of conversations loaded with Biblical quotations and their literal interpretations, this orthodox daughter of an ultra-orthodox theological professor swept away the then current conceptions of heaven, substituting a place of light and love where the dear dead retained their familiar characteristics and all the things that they had loved worthily here. It reads strangely now because of its subject and its method, but it brought solace to many thousands and became one of the most influential works of fiction ever written by an American. The circulation in the USA fell somewhat below 100,000 but was greater in England.

American DNB

**We could both wish that our first impression of Katherine Mansfield was not that she stinks like a — well, civet cat that had taken to street walking. In truth, I'm a little shocked by her commonness at first sight; lines so hard and cheap. However, when this diminishes, she is so intelligent and inscrutable that she repays friendship.

Virginia Woolf, A WRITER'S DIARY

One day when the Sultan was in his palace at Damascus a beautiful youth who was his favourite rushed into his presence, crying out in great agitation that he must fly at once to Baghdad, and imploring leave to borrow his Majesty's swiftest horse.

The Sultan asked why he was in such haste to go to Baghdad. 'Because,' the youth answered, 'as I passed through the gardens of the Palace just now, Death was standing there, and when he saw me he stretched out his arms as if to threaten me, and I must lose no time in escaping from him.'

The young man was given leave to take the Sultan's horse and fly, and when he was gone the Sultan went down indignantly into the garden, and found Death still there. 'How dare you make threatening gestures at my favourite?' he cried; but Death, astonished, answered: 'I assure your Majesty I did not threaten him. I only threw up my arms in surprise at seeing him here, because I have a tryst with him tonight in Baghdad.'

**Edith Wharton,** A Backward Glance[*]

These be
Three silent things:
The Falling snow . . . the hour
Before the dawn . . . the mouth of one
Just dead.

**Adelaide Crapsey,** 'Cinquain: Triad'

Death seems to provide the minds of the Anglo-Saxon race with a greater fund of innocent amusement than any other single subject . . . the tale must be about dead bodies or very wicked people, preferably both, before the Tired Business Man can feel really happy.

**Dorothy L. Sayers,** The Third Omnibus of Crime

---

[*]Edith scribbled from the first. She used to tell how she read her first venture in story-telling to her mother, a story which began with Mrs Brown saying to Mrs Tompkins, 'If only I had known you were going to call I could have tidied up the drawing-room.' To which Lucretia Stevens Rhinelander (her mother) rejoined, 'Drawing-rooms are *always* tidy.'

In the black bitter drizzle, in rain and dirt,
The wreaths are stacked in the factory entrance-yard.
People gather about them. Nobody's hurt
At the rank allusion to death. Down on the hard
Cobblestones go the painted girls on their knees
To read what the football club has put on the card.
There is interest, and delight, and a sense of ease.
Is it only that flowers smell sweet, and are pretty and bright,
Or because of the senseless waste of so many pounds,
Or because in that dreadful place the unwonted sight
Of a heap of blossom is balm to unconscious wounds?

**Ruth Pitter,** 'FUNERAL WREATHS'


Human life consists in mutual service. No grief, pain, misfortune or
'broken heart', is excuse for cutting off one's life while any power of
service remains. But when all usefulness is over, when one is assured of
an unavoidable and imminent death, it is the simplest of human rights
to choose a quick and easy death in place of a slow and horrible one.

**Charlotte Gilman,** note written before her suicide


The tombstone is about the only thing that can stand upright and lie on
its face at the same time.

**Mary Wilson Little**


Holy Moses! Have a look!
Flesh decayed in every nook!
Some rare bits of brain be here
Mortal loads of beef and beer.
. . .

Famous some were – yet they died:
Poets – Statesmen – Rogues beside,
Kings – Queens, all of them do rot,
What about them? Now – they're not!

**Amanda M. Ros,** 'ON VISITING WESTMINSTER
ABBEY'

In some parts of Ireland the sleep which knows no waking is always
followed by a wake which knows no sleeping.

**Mary Wilson Little**


Drink, and dance and laugh and lie,
Love the reeling midnight through,
For tomorrow we shall die!
(But, alas, we never do.)

**Dorothy Parker, 'The Flaw in Paganism'**


Razors pain you;
Rivers are damp;
Acids stain you;
And drugs cause cramp.
Guns aren't lawful;
Nooses give;
Gas smells awful;
You might as well live.

**Dorothy Parker, 'Résumé'**


Nobody heard him, the dead man,
But still he lay moaning:
I was much further out than you thought
And not waving but drowning.

Poor chap, he always loved larking
And now he's dead
It must have been too cold for him his heart gave way,
They said.

Oh, no no no, it was too cold always
(Still the dead one lay moaning)
I was much too far out all my life
And not waving but drowning.

**Stevie Smith, 'Not Waving but Drowning'**

# Acknowledgements

Grateful acknowledgement is due to the authors and publishers listed below (and where indicated to the author's literary agent or executors) for permission to reproduce extracts from the following works of prose or poetry or in some instances entire poems.

Every effort has been made to trace copyright holders of material in this book. The publishers apologize if any material has been included without permission and would be glad to be told of anyone who has not been consulted.

CHRISTABEL ABERCONWAY: From *A Wiser Woman?* By permission of Hutchinson Publishing Group Limited. RUTH ADAM: From *A woman's place 1910–1975.* Copyright © 1977 by Ruth Adam. Reprinted by permission of W. W. Norton & Company, Inc. SUSAN MARY ALSOP: From *Lady Sackville: A Biography.* Copyright © 1978 by Susan Mary Alsop. Reprinted by permission of Doubleday & Company, Inc. ELIZABETH von ARMIN: From *Elizabeth and Her German Garden* and *The Enchanted April.* Reprinted by permission of Ann E. Hardham. ENID BAGNOLD: From *Autobiography.* Copyright © 1969 by Enid Bagnold. Reprinted by permission of Brandt & Brandt Literary Agents, Inc. BERYL BAINBRIDGE: From *The Bottle Factory Outing,* published by Gerald Duckworth & Co. Ltd. NINA BAWDEN: From *A Woman of My Age.* Copyright © 1967 by Nina Bawden. Reprinted by permission of the Author and her Agent, James Brown Associates, Inc. SIMONE de BEAUVOIR: From *The Second Sex,* translated by H. M. Parshley. Copyright 1952 by Alfred A. Knopf, Inc. Reprinted by permission of Alfred A. Knopf, Inc. MOLLY BERKELEY: From *Winking at the Brim.* Copyright © 1967 by the Countess of Berkeley. Reprinted by permission of Houghton Mifflin Company. ENID BLYTON: From *Malory Towers,* published by Methuen Children's Books Ltd. PHYLLIS BOTTOME: From *Search for a Soul,* published by Faber and Faber Ltd., by permission of David Higham Associates. ELIZABETH BOWEN: From *The Death of the Heart.* Copyright 1938 and renewed 1966 by Elizabeth D. C. Cameron. Reprinted by permission of Alfred A. Knopf, Inc. ANGELA BRAZIL: From *A Patriotic Schoolgirl,* published by Blackie & Son Ltd. DORITA FAIRLIE BRUCE: From *Dimsie Grows Up,* published by Oxford University Press. PEARL S. BUCK: From *Advice to Unborn Novelists,* published by Methuen & Co. Ltd. By permission of Harold Ober Associates. BARBARA CARTLAND: From *We Danced All Night* and *A Virgin in Paris,* published by Hurst & Blackett Ltd. By permission of Rupert Crew Ltd. WILLA CATHER: From *Willa Cather on Writing: Critical Studies on Writing as an Art.* Copyright 1949 by The Executors of the Estate of Willa Cather. Reprinted by permission of Alfred A. Knopf, Inc. COLETTE: From *The Vagabond,* translated by Enid McLead. Copyright © 1955 by Farrar, Straus and Young (now Farrar, Straus & Giroux, Inc.). Reprinted by permission of Farrar, Straus & Giroux, Inc.

FRANCES CORNFORD: From "London Spring" and "To A Fat Lady" from *Collected Poems* 1954. From "A Child's Dream" and the poem "In A Fruitful Land." All reprinted by permission of The Cressett Press. RICHMAL CROMPTON: From *Just William*, published by William Collins Sons & Co. Ltd. By permission of A. P. Watt Ltd. ELIZABETH DAVID: From *French Provincial Cooking*, published by Michael Joseph Ltd. Used by permission of David Higham Associates Limited. ELIZABETH GOULD DAVIS: From *The First Sex*. Copyright © 1971 by Elizabeth Gould Davis. All Rights Reserved. Reprinted by permission of Joan Daves. E. M. DELAFIELD: From *Diary of a Provincial Lady*, published by Howard Baker Press Ltd. Reprinted by permission of A D Peters & Co Ltd. ISAK DINESEN: From *Seven Gothic Tales*. Copyright 1934 by Harrison Smith and Robert Haas, Inc. and renewed 1962 by Isak Dinesen. Reprinted by permission of Random House, Inc. MARGARET DRABBLE: From *A Summer Bird-Cage*, published by George Weidenfeld & Nicolson Ltd. By permission of A. P. Watt Ltd. ELAINE DUNDY: From *The Dud Avocado*, published by Victor Gollancz Ltd. NELL DUNN: From *Up the Junction* and *Poor Cow*. Used by permission of the Author. DAPHNE FIELDING: From *Emerald and Nancy*, published by Eyre & Spottiswoode Ltd. By permission of Curtis Brown Ltd. JANET FLANNER (Genet): From *Paris Was Yesterday, 1925–1939*, edited by Irving Drutman. Copyright © 1972 by Janet Flanner. Reprinted by permission of The Viking Press. MARGARET FORSTER: From *The Seduction of Mrs. Pendlebury*. Used by permission of Curtis Brown Ltd., London. ANTONIA FRASER: From *My Oxford*, published by Robson Books. BETTY FRIEDAN: From *The Feminine Mystique*. Copyright © 1963 by Betty Friedan. Reprinted by permission of W. W. Norton & Company, Inc. MARTHA GELHORN: From *Weekend at Grimsby*, published by Andre Deutsch Ltd. STELLA GIBBONS: From *Cold Comfort Farm*, published by Longman. By permission of David Higham Associates. GERMAINE GREER: From *The Female Eunuch*. Copyright © 1971 by Germaine Greer. Used with the permission of McGraw-Hill Book Company. JOYCE GRENFELL: From *Stately as a Galleon*. Used by permission of Richard Scott Simon Limited.

RADCLYFFE HALL: From *The Well of Loneliness*. Used by permission of Hutchinson Publishing Group Limited. ROBERT HENREY, Mrs.: From *Paloma*. Used by permission of J. M. Dent & Sons Ltd. and the Author. BEA HOWE: From *Child in Chile*. Used by permission of Hughes Massie Limited. M.V. HUGHES: From *A London Child of the 1880's*, published by Oxford University Press. ELIZABETH JENKINS: From *The Tortoise and the Hare* and *Elizabeth the Great*. Copyright 1958, 1959 by Elizabeth Jenkins. Reprinted by permission of Victor Gollancz, Ltd. and Curtis Brown, Ltd. ELIZABETH JENNINGS: "One Flesh" from *Collected Poems*, published by Macmillan Publishers Ltd. Reprinted by permission of David Higham Associates Limited. F. TENNYSON JESSE: From *The Lacquer Lady*, published by Virago Ltd. PAMELA HANSFORD JOHNSON: From *Night and Silence Who Is Here?* Copyright ©1963 by Pamela Hansford Johnson. Reprinted by permission of Curtis Brown, Ltd. From *Cork Street Next to the Hatters*, reprinted by permission of Curtis Brown Ltd., London ERICA JONG: From *Fear of Flying*. Copyright © 1973 by Erica Mann Jong. Reprinted by permission of Holt, Rinehart and Winston, Publishers. VIVA KING: From *The Weeping and the Laughter*, published by Macdonald & Janes Publishers. By permission of Hope Leresche & Sayle. MARGARET LANE: From *The Tale of Beatrix Potter*. Used by permission of Frederick Warne & Co., Ldt. FRAN LEBOWITZ: From *Metropolitan Life*. Copyright © 1974, 1975, 1976, 1977, 1978 by Fran Lebowitz. Reprinted by permission of the publisher, E. P. Dutton. COLE LESLEY: From *Remembered Laughter: The Life of Noel Coward*. Copyright 1976 by Cole Lesley. Reprinted by permission of Alfred A.

Knopf, Inc. DORIS LESSING: From *The Grass Is Singing,* published by Thomas Y. Crowell. Copyright © 1950, 1978 by Doris Lessing. By permission of Harper & Row, Publishers, Inc. ADA LEVERSON: From *Love at Second Sight,* by permission of Francis Wyndham. ANNE MORROW LINDBERG: From *Listen! The Wind,* by permission of Harcourt Brace Jovanovich, Inc., publisher. MARY MacCARTHY: From *A Nineteenth-Century Childhood,* published by Hamish Hamilton Ltd. By permission of Lady David Cecil. ROSE MACAULAY: From *Personal Pleasures,* published by Victor Gollancz Ltd., from *Crewe Train,* published by William Collins Sons & Co., Ltd., from "Driving Sheep." By permission of A D Peters & Co., Ltd. F. M. MAYOR: From *The Rector's Daughter,* published by Penguin Books Limited. By permission of David Mayor. CARSON McCULLERS: From "Relections in a Golden." Copyright 1941 by Carson McCullers. From "The Ballad of the Sad Cafe." Copyright 1951 by Carson McCullers. Both from *The Shorter Novels and Stories of Carson McCullers.* Reprinted by permission of Houghton Mifflin Company. PHYLLIS McGINLEY: "Trial and Error" from *A Short Walk from the Station.* Copyright 1934 by Phyllis McGinley. Copyright renewed © 1962 by Phyllis McGinley. Reprinted by permission of Viking Penguin Inc. IRENE RUTHERFORD McLEOD: From "Lone Dog" from *Songs to Save a Soul.* Copyright 1915 by Irene Rutherford McLeod. Reprinted by permission of Viking Penguin Inc. EDNA ST. VINCENT MILLAY: "The buck in the Snow," excerpts from "To the Not Impossible Him," and "The Englishman foxtrots as he fox-hunts" from *Collected Poems,* Harper & Row. Copyright 1922, 1924, 1928, 1950, 1951, 1955 by Edna St. Vincent Millay and Norma Millay Ellis. Used by permission of Norma Millay Ellis, Literary Executor. JULIET MITCHELL: From *Woman's Estate.* Copyright © 1971 by Juliet Mitchell. Reprinted by permission of Pantheon Books, a division of Random House, Inc. NANCY MITFORD: From *The Blessing* and *Love in a Cold Climate,* published by Hamish Hamilton Ltd. Reprinted by permission of A D Peters & Co Ltd. DIAN MOSLEY: From *A Life of Contrasts,* published by Hamish Hamilton Ltd. DERVLA MURPHY: From *On a Shoe String to Coorg,* published by John Murray Ltd. VENETIA MURRAY: From *Twelve Days of Christmas,* published by William Collins Sons & Co., Ltd. By permission of Curtis Brown, Ltd. ALVA MYRIAL and VERA KLEIN: From *Women's Two Roles.* Reprinted by permission of Humanities Press, New Jersey. EDITH OLIVIER: From *Without Knowing Mr. Walkley.* Used by permission of Rosemary Olivier. DOROTHY PARKER: "Resume" from *The Lovely Leave,* and "The Flaw in Paganism" from *The Portable Dorothy Parker.* Copyright 1926, renewed 1954 by Dorothy Parker. Copyright 1931, © renewed 1959 by Dorothy Parker. Reprinted by permission of Viking Penguin Inc. RUTH PITTER: From "Funeral Wreaths" from *Poems 1926–1966.* From "A Mountainous Country" from *Urania.* By permission of The Cresset Press. BEATRIS POTTER: From The Tale of Ginger and Pickles, The Tailor of Gloucester, The Tale of Samuel Whiskers, By permission of Frederick Warne & Co. BARBARA PYM: From *Less Than Angels* and *Jane and Prudence,* published by Jonathan Cape Ltd. By permission of the Estate of Barbara Pym. GWEN RAVERAT: From *Period Piece,* published by Faber and Faber, Ltd. V. SACKVILLE-WEST: From "Sissinghurst," published by Hogarth Press Ltd. By permission of Nigel Nicolson. From "The Land" by permission of Doubleday & Company, Inc. DOROTHY L. SAYERS: From "Lord, I thank Thee–" in *London Calling,* edited by Storm Jameson. Copyright 1942 by Harper & Row, Publishers, Inc. Reprinted by permission of the publisher. CLARE SHERIDAN: From *To The Four Winds,* published by Andre Deutsch Ltd. Used by permission of David Higham Associates Limited. EDITH SITWELL: From *The English Eccentrics.* Used by permission of Dennis Dobson Publishers.

ELIZABETH SMART: From *By Grand Central Station I Sat Down and Wept,* published by Polytantric Press. STEVIE SMITH: "Not Waving But Drowning," from "The Singing Cat," and from "Autumn" from *Selected Poems of Stevie Smith.* Copyright © 1964 by Stevie Smith. Reprinted by permission of New Directions. "The Past," "Be Off, "Wretched Woman," "This Englishwoman," and from "Mrs. Simpkins" from *Collected Poems.* Copyright © 1976 by James MacGibbon. Reprinted by permission of Oxford University Press, Inc. From *Novel on Yellow Paper,* published by Virago Ltd. By permission of James MacGibbon, Executor. MURIEL SPARK: From *Memento Mori.* Copyright © 1958 by Administration Anstalt. Reprinted by permission of Harold Ober Associates. FREYA STARK: From *Traveller's Prelude,* published by John Murray Ltd. By permission of Hope Leresche & Sayle. GERTRUDE STEIN: From *The Autobiography of Alice B. Toklas* published by Penguin Books Limited. By permission of David High Associates Limited. ELIZABETH TAYLOR: From *Blaming, The Soul of Kindness,* and *At. Mrs. Lippincote's.* By permission of A. M. Heath & Company Ltd. for the Estate of Elizabeth Taylor. FLORA THOMPSON: From *Lark Rise to Candleford,* published by Oxford University Press. By permission of Hope Leresche & Sayle. JUDITH VIORST: "True Love" and "Divorce." Copyright © 1968 by Judith Viorst. From *It's Hard to be Hip Over Thirty.* Used by permission of The Lescher Agency. SYLVIA TOWNSEND WARNER: From "Under New Management" and "A Kitchen Knife" from *Winter in the Air.* From "English Climate" from *Museum of Cheats.* Used by permission of Chatto and Windus Ltd., Susanna Pinney, and William Maxwell. HILDA WAUGHAN: From *Her Father's House,* published by William Heinemann Ltd. By permission of Hope Leresche & Sayle. FAY WELDON: From *Down Among the Women,* reprinted by permission of St. Martin's Press, Inc. KATHARINE WHITEHORN: From *Roundabout,* published by Eyre Methuen Ltd. Reprinted by permission of A D Peters & Co Ltd. BARBARA WILSON: From *The House of Memories,* reprinted by permission of Peter and Sir Martin Wilson. VIRGINIA WOOLF: From *A Room of One's Own, Night and Day, A Writer's Diary,* and *To the Lighthouse.* Used by permission of Harcourt Brace Jovanovich, Inc., publisher. ELINOR WYLIE: From "Portrait in Black Paint, With a Very Sparing Use of Whitewash" and from "Nonsense Rhyme" from *Collected Poems of Elinor Wylie.* Copyright 1932 by Alfred A. Knopf, Inc. and renewed 1960 by Edwina C. Rubenstein. Reprinted by permission of Alfred A. Knopf, Inc.

# Biographical Index

This index is intended to help the reader, in a light-hearted way, to place the contributors in their correct social and historical setting. If the author is too well known to require further comment the dates of birth and death alone are given. Some readers may think that, on this basis, much of the information given is superfluous. It should, however, be borne in mind that what is common knowledge on one side of the Atlantic is not necessarily so on the other. In a few instances, mainly when the author has been quoted from a secondary source, we have been unable to discover any biographical details, for which we can only apologise. In others, the allusion in the main text makes further comment unnecessary. Since the publishers hope that this book will run to many editions, any missing information which readers can supply will be warmly welcome. Dates of living authors have for the most part been omitted.

## A

**Aberconway, Lady (1890-1974).** 'Christabel surrounded herself with beauty. Her life was spent in giving and enjoying pleasure.' 79, 121, 186

**Ace, Jane.** Quoted in Goodman Ace, *The Fine Art of Hypochondria.* 66

**Adam, Ruth.** British writer; author of *A Woman's Place 1910-1975.* 173, 207

**Alcott, Louisa May (1832-1888).** American novelist and poet; author of *Little Women.* 'The American home with its teapots and curtains, its centripetal and protective femininity, appears in her work with the vividness and detail of a Currier & Ives print.' 154

**Alexander, Cecil Frances (1818-95).** Author of many universally known hymns, including 'There is a green hill far away', 'All things bright and beautiful' and 'Once in royal David's city'; her husband became Protestant Archbishop of Armagh, Primate of all Ireland and was one-time professor of poetry at Oxford. 211

**Alsop, Susan Mary.** American biographer; formerly married to a US diplomat; wrote *To Marietta From Paris,* based on her correspondence with Marietta Tree. 123

**Anderson, Elizabeth Garrett (1836-1917).** Pioneer of the movement to include women in the medical profession. In 1908 she was elected Mayor of Aldeburgh, thus becoming the first woman mayor in England. 174

**Arnim, Countess von (1866-1941).** Born in Sydney, Australia, she was a cousin of Katherine Mansfield. Her second husband was the 2nd Earl Russell, elder brother of Bertrand. 85, 86, 121

**Ashford, Daisy (1882-1972).** Author of *The Young Visiters,* which some believed was actually the work of Sir James Barrie. 50, 72, 120, 125, 128, 192

**Asquith, Margot (1864-1945).** Second wife of H. H. Asquith, Prime Minister 1908-16; well known for her tactlessness. 20, 75, 183

**Atherton, Gertrude (1857-1948).** American novelist; Henry James found both Gertrude and her work 'unbearably vulgar'. 84, 178

**Austen, Jane (1775-1815).** 38, 40, 45, 72, 78, 84, 85, 87, 99, 100, 122, 151, 157, 203, 210

## B

**Bagnold, Enid (b. 1889).** English novelist and playwright; was married to Sir Roderick Jones (d. 1962), principal proprietor of Reuters. Her best known novel is *National Velvet.* 42, 57, 96

**Bainbridge, Beryl (b. 1934).** English novelist of rare and original wit. 21

Barbauld, Anna Letitia (1743-1825). English author. 'Mrs Barbauld's masterly command of English has been matched by few other writers for children.' 212

Barclay, Florence (1862-1921). Sentimental novelist. 'In 1912 Mrs Barclay received a blow on the head; a cerebral haemorrhage threatened to put an end to her writing, but another opportune accident, when she was hit on the head by an oar, while boating on the lake at Keswick, restored her productivity.' 'Nobody else can write a silly story half so well as she . . . Though on all sides the blood rains down in torrents, love's interests still are in safe hands with Florence.' (J. C. Squire). 39

Baum, Vicki (1888-1960). Born in Austria but lived in USA after 1931. Her best known work is *Grand Hotel*. 53

Bawden, Nina (b. 1925). English novelist. 206

Beausobre, Iulia de. Russian 'political' prisoner in the 1930s; escaped to England. 148

Beauvoir, Simone de (b. 1908). French existentialist writer and friend of Jean-Paul Sartre. Her novel, *The Mandarins*, won the Prix Goncourt in 1954. 37, 41, 94

Beers, Ethel Lynn (1827-79). American poet; had a premonition that she would die immediately after the appearance of her collected poems. *All Quiet on the Potomac Tonight and Other Poems* was published on 10 October 1879. She died the following day. 213

Beeton, Isabella Mary (1836-65). She was only 25 when her colossal *Book of Household Management* appeared. Her biography, by her great-niece, Nancy Spain, was published in 1956. 104

Behn, Aphra (1640-89). English dramatist and novelist; spent part of her childhood in Surinam; worked as a British spy in Antwerp but was not paid and ended in a debtor's gaol; thereafter she wrote for a living; a hard-working hack who could turn out bawdier plays than any man. 78, 79, 81, 101, 151

Benson, Stella (1892-1933). English novelist who spent much of her short life in China. The only work of hers which received wide acclaim was *Tobit Transplanted*. 54

Berkeley, Molly. Second wife of 8th and last Earl of Berkeley; born Mary Lowell in Boston, Mass. 55, 194

Blavatsky, Elena (1831-91). Religious crank who founded the Theosophical Society in 1875. 153

Blessington, Countess of (1789-1849). Beautiful Irish girl of respectable but impoverished background who became one of London's leading hostesses but died bankrupt in Paris. 62, 151

Blyton, Enid (d. 1968). English writer of children's books, responsible, among other crimes, for Noddy and The Famous Five. 31

Bonham Carter, Lady Violet (1887-1969). Elder daughter of H. H. Asquith; prominent in Liberal politics for many years; mother-in-law of Jo Grimond; created a life peeress, 1964. 193

Bottome, Phyllis (1884-1963). Novelist; daughter of an American clergyman and an English mother. 29, 30

Bowen, Elizabeth (1899-1973). Anglo-Irish novelist whose work is ranked, by some, with that of Virginia Woolf and Katherine Mansfield. 36, 128, 135

Brazil, Angela (1869-1947). Captain of the 'Jolly Hockeysticks' team of writers of school stories for girls. 32, 187

Brittain, Vera (1893-1970). English essayist and novelist, best known for her *Testament of Youth* (1933), serialised on television in 1979. 72

Brontë, Charlotte (1816-55). Wrote *Jane Eyre, Shirley* and *Villette*. 28, 47, 121

Brontë, Emily (1818-48). Wrote *Wuthering Heights*. 71, 140, 152

Browning, Elizabeth Barrett (1806-61). 20, 57, 85, 152, 204

Bruce, Dorita Fairlie (1885-1947). 'The well-ordered life of many girls' private schools is convincingly conveyed through descriptions of regular music practices, and walks in crocodile, of girls discarding gymslips for silk dresses on special occasions, or standing around for hours on the boundary, fielding at cricket matches.' 32, 77, 181

Buck, Pearl S. (1892-1973). American novelist; winner of the Nobel Prize for Literature 1938. Her best known novel, *The Good Earth* (1931), now seems to have been somewhat overrated. 161

Burney, Fanny (1752-1840). English novelist and diarist; became Mme D'Arblay after her marriage to a French general. 124, 200

Butler, Josephine (1828-1906). English social reformer who established homes for fallen women. 174

# C

**Campbell, Mrs Patrick** (1867-1940). A famous actress who made her name as 'The Second Mrs Tanqueray'. She o..ed much to the patronage of the Prince of Wales. 57

**Carlyle, Jane** (1801-66). Wife of Thomas Carlyle. It was said of them that it was fortunate they married each other, thereby making two people miserable instead of four. 212

**Cartland, Barbara.** Phenomenally prolific romantic novelist; mother of the ex-Lady Lewisham (q.v.).47,52,79,175

**Cather, Willa** (1875-1945). American novelist; her work has been summarised as 'grave, flexible, a little austere, wonderfully transparent, everywhere economical.' 89, 139, 146, 162, 167

**Catherine II of Russia** (1729-96).Usually known as Catherine the Great. 190

**Chase, Ilka** (b. 1905). American author and actress; was once married to Louis Calhern. 179

**Churchill, Sarah, Duchess of Marlborough** (1660-1744). Intimate friend and confidante of Queen Anne. 190

**Churchill, Lady Randolph** (1854-1951). American, née Jennie Jerome, mother of Winston Churchill. 204

**Cleghorn, Sarah Norcliffe** (1876-1957). American pacifist, socialist, anti-vivisectionist. 23, 145

**Cockburn, Alison** (1712-94). Achieved fame solely as the author of one short ballad, 'I've Seen the Smiling of Fortune Beguiling'; Walter Scott, at the age of six, said, 'I like her because she is a virtuoso like myself.' 145

**Coffey, Denise** (b. 1936). English actress; her favourite part is that of Cecily Bumtrinket. 81

**Colette** (1873-1954). French novelist. When she died she was given a state funeral, the only honour of its kind to be given to a woman writer in the history of all the four republics and the highest posthumous honour a citizen can receive. 31, 66, 80, 101

**Compton-Burnett, Ivy** (1884-1969). English novelist of whose work Elizabeth Bowen said, 'Costume and accessories play so little part that her characters sometimes give the effect of being physically, as well as psychologically, in the nude, and of not only standing and moving about in but actually sitting on thin air.' 149, 163, 207

**Cook, Eliza** (1818-89). English poet, wrote 'The Old Armchair'; 'she was extremely popular with the semi-educated'. 28

**Coolidge, Susan,** pen-name of **Sarah Chauncey Woolsey** (1835-1905). Famous as author of *What Katy Did*. Blessed with a large body and a swinging gait, she was once described as 'a cross between an elephant and a butterfly'. 110

**Cooper, Lettice** (b.1897). Distinguished Yorkshire novelist. Has also written many children's books, biographies, works of literary criticism, and appreciations of the Yorkshire countryside. Recently received the O.B.E. in her 81st year. 116

**Cornford, Frances** (1886-1960). Won the Heinemann Poetry Prize 1948, Queen's Medal for Poetry 1959; granddaughter of Charles Darwin. 111, 134, 138, 139, 163

**Courtney, Margaret** (1822-62). American poet. 18

**Cowan, Annabel** 166

**Crowley, Hannah** (1743-1809). English dramatist; her greatest success was *The Belle's Stratagem*. 180

**Crapsey, Adelaide** (1878-1914). American poet; originator of the cinquain, a 5-line unrhyming stanza, containing respectively 2, 4, 6, 8 and 2 syllables. 215

**Crompton, Richmal** (1890-1969). Author of the 'William' books which have sold in excess of 10 million copies. 33, 88, 194

**Curtis, Lilian.** An American contemporary of Julia Moore (q.v.). The poem is quoted in Jack Loudan's *O Rare Amanda!* 43

# D

**Dache, Lily** 95

**Dallas, Mary Kyle** (1837-97). American poet and novelist. 54

**Daudet, Mme Léon.** Wife of the son of Alphonse Daudet. 105

**David, Elizabeth.** Famous English writer on cooking. 105

**Deffand, Mme du** (1697-1780). Remembered mainly for her friendship and correspondence with famous men, particularly Voltaire, Montesquieu and Horace Walpole. 179

**Delafield, E. M.** (1890-1943). Pen-name of Elizabeth Dashwood, English novelist and daughter of Mrs de la Pasture. Her husband was agent to Mrs Adams of Bradfield, Devon, 'Lady B.' in *The Provincial Lady*. 29, 31, 138, 150, 167

**Delaney, Shelagh (b. 1936).** English playwright who rocketed to fame in 1958 when *A Taste of Honey* appeared. Not much has been heard from her since. 173

**Diane de Poitiers, Duchesse de Valentinois (1499-1566).** Mistress of Henry II of France. 203

**Dickinson, Emily (1830-86).** American poet. 70, 146, 211

**Diller, Phyllis (b. 1917).** American writer and actress. 23, 66

**Dinesen, Isak (1885-1962).** Danish writer whose real name was Karen Blixen. Lived for many years in Kenya where her native servants thought she was writing a new Koran. 40, 86, 172

**Dix, Dorothy;** pseudonym of **Elizabeth Meriwether Gilmer (1870-1951).** American journalist; writer of a famous column of advice to the lovelorn. 62

**Dodge, Mary Abigail (1836-96).** Ardent American feminist. 163

**Douglas-Home, Lady Caroline (b. 1937).** Daughter of Lord Home, Prime Minister 1963-4. 194

**Drabble, Margaret (b. 1939).** English novelist whose works are particularly remarkable for the perceptive analysis of the backgrounds against which they are set. 93

**Drake, Leah Bodine.** American poet. 115

**Draper, Ruth (1884-1956).** American *diseuse*, granddaughter of the famous newspaper editor, Charles A. Dana. 24, 128, 149, 168

**Duncan, Isadora (1878-1927).** American dancer of whom Rodin said that he sometimes felt she was the greatest woman the world had ever known. 22, 147

**Dundy, Elaine.** American writer of great wit and charm; was once married to Kenneth Tynan, theatre critic. 97, 107, 159

**Dunn, Nell (b. 1936).** Very rich English writer, particularly concerned with the urban poor. 18, 38, 51

# E

**Eastwood, Dorothea (d. 1961).** 25

**Eddy, Mary Baker (1821-1910).** Founder of the Christian Science Church. 147

**Eden, Clarissa (b.1920).** Married 1st Earl of Avon (Sir Anthony Eden). 194

**Edgeworth, Maria (1809-92).** The second of her father's 21 children! Her collaboration with her father in the production of *Practical Education* marks a definite step in the development of education to which due tribute is seldom paid; it was the first work in which cognisance was taken of the workings of a child's mind. 99

**Ekland, Britt.** An actress of Scandinavian origin, once married to Peter Sellers. 50

**Eliot, George (1819-80).** Pen-name of Mary Ann Evans. 28, 55, 84, 92, 101, 112, 122, 164, 168, 178, 180, 200, 204, 211

**Elizabeth, Queen, the Queen Mother (b. 1900).** Lord Warden of the Cinque Ports. 186, 193

**Elizabeth II, H. M. Queen (b. 1926).** 192

**Evans, Dame Edith (1888-1976).** Distinguished English actress renowned for her resonant voice. 181

# F

**Fawcett, Dame Millicent (1847-1929).** Leader of the women's suffrage movement; sister of Elizabeth Garrett Anderson. 177

**Ferber, Edna (1887-1968).** American author; wrote the original book of *Showboat;* member of the Algonquin Round Table. 35, 206

**Fey, Imogene** 19

**Fielding, Daphne (b. 1904).** English biographer; daughter of Lord Vivian; once married to the Marquess of Bath; has written biographies of Rosa Lewis and Iris Tree. 125, 205

**Fishback, Margaret (b. 1904).** American poet. 100

**Flanner, Janet (b. 1892).** Foreign correspondent for *The New Yorker*. 95

**Fleming, Marjorie** 114

**Ford, Lena Guilbert (d. 1916).** American poet killed in an air raid on London during the First World War. 185

**Forster, Margaret (b. 1938).** English novelist; author of *Georgy Girl;* married to the journalist, Hunter Davies. 65

**Fraser, Antonia (b. 1932).** English historian; daughter of Lord Longford. 106, 149

**Frederick, Pauline (1883-1938).** American stage and screen actress known as 'the aristocratic vampire of the screen'. 180

**Friedan, Betty.** Ardent feminist. 174

**Hull, Ethel Maude.** 'It was E. M. Hull who, with *The Sheik* in 1919, first put the desert on the map as a good place for sex . . . (Her heroine's) adventures were possibly a compensation for (her) own lack of amorous excitement, for she was married tò a dull pig-breeder called Percy.' 77

**Hull, Josephine.** Actress. 158

# J

**Jekyll, Agnes Lady (1861-1937).** Wife of a distinguished civil servant, she devoted most of her time to good works. 20

**Jenkins, Elizabeth.** English writer; has written biographies of Queen Elizabeth I, Lady Caroline Lamb, Jane Austen. 29, 84

**Jennings, Elizabeth (b. 1926).** English poet and translator of Michelangelo's sonnets. 205

**Jesse, Fryniwid Tennyson (1889-1958).** English novelist and playwright; great-niece of Alfred, Lord T. Her remarkable novel, *The Lacquer Lady,* tells how the jilting of a Burmese girl by a French merchant led to the annexation of Upper Burma by the British. 31

**Johnson, Pamela Hansford (b. 1912).** English author; wife of C. P. Snow. 88, 124, 128, 160, 179

**Jones, Constance** 124

**Jones, Thelma Hamilton** 33

**Jong, Erica.** American novelist; author of *Fear of Flying.* 53, 55

# K

**Kerr, Jean (b. 1923).** American author and playwright. 97, 104, 198

**Kilgallen, Dorothy (1913-65).** Hollywood gossip-writer, journalist and American TV personality. 101

**Kilmer, Aline (1888-1944).** American poet, wife of Joyce Kilmer. 23

**King, Viva (1893-1979).** London hostess of the literary and artistic world. 30

**Knox, Cleonie,** pseudonym of **Magdalen King-Hall (1904-71).** 201

**Klein, Dr Viola.** English feminist and sociologist; author of *The Feminine Character.* 175

# L

**Landon, Letitia Elizabeth (1802-38).** English poet and novelist; wrote *Castruccio Castracani,* described as a tragedy! Died from drinking prussic acid at Cape Coast Castle, of which her husband was governor. 40, 69

**Luce, Clare Booth (b. 1903).** American playwright; former Congresswoman; US Ambassador to Rome, 1953-7; 'She writes of the rich and for the rich but she always gives them hell; her women are sluts, backbiters or dumb-bells, her men are androgynes, lechers or sots.' 154

**Lane, Margaret (b. 1907).** English novelist and biographer. Her life of Beatrix Potter is a model of its kind. 20, 162

**Lebowitz, Fran.** American journalist optimistically described as another Dorothy Parker. 20, 36, 105, 106, 113

**Lee, Emma** 57

**Lee, Vernon (1865-1935).** Pen-name of Violet Paget, English novelist and writer on aesthetics, politics and Italian art. She wrote over forty books as well as a puppet show called *The Prince of the Hundred Soups.* 163

**Lessing, Doris (b. 1919).** English novelist; she spent her childhood on a farm in Rhodesia. 201, 204

**Leszcinska, Marie (1703-68).** Daughter of Stanislas of Poland; wife of Louix XV of France. 190

**Letts, Winifred M. (1882-1972).** Irish novelist and playwright. 113

**Leverson, Ada (1862-1933).** Her skill as a novelist has been utterly and unjustly forgotten. She is now only remembered for her friendship with Oscar Wilde. 21, 30, 62, 63

**Lewis, Rosa (1867-1952).** Ran the Cavendish Hotel in Jermyn Street; was the subject of a recent TV series. 75

**Lewisham, Lady (b. 1929).** Daughter of Barbara Cartland; now married to the Earl Spencer. 95

**Lindbergh, Anne Morrow (b. 1906).** Wife of Charles Lindbergh, who made the first solo non-stop transatlantic flight; she has written several books, including *North to the Orient* and *Listen, the Wind.* 130, 197

**Little, Mary Wilson.** American writer.

**Loos, Anita (b. 1893).** American writer of novels, films and plays who epitomised the Roaring Twenties, the John Held cartoon, the flapper and the raccoon coat. 72, 198

# M

**Macaulay, Rose (1889-1958).** English

novelist, more regarded as a satirist than she might have wished. 33, 37, 134, 137, 162

MacCarthy, Mary. Daughter of Francis Warre-Cornish, Vice-Provost of Eton; married Sir Desmond MacCarthy, the foremost literary critic of his day; mother-in-law of Lord David Cecil. 193

McCarthy, Mary (b. 1912). American writer whose novels 'are remarkable for their lucid style, accompanied by an acute wit equipped with the malice to propel it'. 39, 200

McCullers, Carson (1917-67). American novelist who wrote very little, all of it excellent. 64, 100

MacDonald, Betty (1908-58). American humorous writer. Her book, *The Egg and I,* sold over a million copies. 86

McGinley, Phyllis (b. 1905). American writer of light verse and books for children. 154, 180

McLeod, Irene Rutherford (b. 1891). English poet; was married to Aubrey de Selincourt. 111

Mansfield, Katherine (1889-1923). Short-story writer born in New Zealand; married to John Middleton Murry. 214

Marbury, Elizabeth 180

Maria Theresa (1717-80). Archduchess of Austria; daughter, wife and mother of Holy Roman Emperors; also mother of Marie-Antoinette. 160

Martineau, Harriet (1802-76). English novelist and economist; born without the senses of smell or taste, she was also deaf; a self-complacent busybody and a prig. 213

Matthews, Mrs 159

Mayor, F. M. (1872-1932). English novelist; her masterpiece, *The Rector's Daughter,* though reputedly not autobiographical, bears a remarkable similarity to the story of her own life. 120, 124

Meynell, Alice (1847-1922). Younger sister of Lady Butler, the painter; was seriously advocated for the Poet Laureateship when Tennyson died, especially by Coventry Patmore. Theodore Maynard said of her, 'All her essays are touched with the spirit of poetry and all her poetry with the spirit of essays.' 70, 96

Millay, Edna St Vincent (1892-1950). American poet of whom it was said that she was the most popular poet of her day, certainly the only one who could live well by writing. 61, 69, 116, 167, 198, 201

Miller, Alice Duer (1874-1942). American novelist and poet; her greatest success, *The White Cliffs,* a long narrative poem extolling Britain's resistance in the Second World War, was turned down by several publishers but became a runaway best-seller after a reading on the wireless by Lynn Fontanne. 199

Miller, Ruth. South African poet. 115

Mitchell, Juliet. English sociologist; author of *Psychoanalysis and Feminism.* 18

Mitford, Nancy (1904-1973). English humorous writer and very U historian. 29, 36, 46, 62, 110, 122, 152, 168, 187, 192

Montagu, Lady Mary Wortley (1689-1762). Eldest daughter of the 5th Earl of Kingston. Her husband was made Ambassador to the Sublime Porte in 1716, whence she brought the practice of inoculation (not vaccination) back to England. 37, 38, 50, 92

Montessori, Maria (1870-1952). Italian educationalist. 27, 28, 147

Montgomery, Roselle Mercier (1874-1933). American writer. 153

Morgan, Constance 140

Moore, Julia A. (1847-1920). American poet. 164

More, Hannah (1745-1833). Religious writer and bluestocking; involved in the establishment of Sunday Schools and The Religious Tract Society. 28, 178

Mosley, Diana (b. 1910). Wife of Sir Oswald Mosley and sister of Nancy Mitford (q.v.). 47, 54

Mulock, Dinah Maria (1826-87). English novelist of Irish extraction; author of *John Halifax, Gentleman;* married George Craik, a partner in the firm of Macmillan & Co. 22, 88

Mumford, Ethel Watts (1878-1940). American writer. 87, 99

Murphy, Dervla. Irish traveller, and writer of enviable charm and wit. To select one title from her *oeuvre* seems presumptuous, but *Full Tilt* certainly deserved a wider public. 55

Murdoch, Iris (b. 1919). English novelist; the abstruse philosophical theories that underlie her novels should not deter one from reading them as rattling good yarns. 51

Murray, Venetia. Granddaughter of Gilbert Murray and one of the most beautiful debs of the fifties. Author of several witty but essentially melancholy novels. 80

**Myrdal, Alva.** Swedish feminist and sociologist. 175

# N

**Nesbit, Edith (1858-1924).** English novelist, poet and writer of children's books; she was married to Herbert Bland and with him helped to found the Fabian Society. 134

**Nicolson, Adela (1865-1904).** Wrote poetry under the pen-name of Laurence Hope because 'the note of passion, expressed in a medium of Oriental temperament and imagery,' would have been thought unsuitable in the wife of an Indian Army general. She wrote 'Pale Hands I Loved Beside the Shalimar'. 153

**Nightingale, Florence (1820-1910).** Very English nurse, hospital reformer and ladies' lady. 174

# O

**O'Brien, Edna (b.1936).** Irish novelist. 201

**Ogilvy, Mrs David** 20

**Olivier, Edith (1879-1948).** English writer who used to say that if she died without meeting Arthur Walkley, dramatic critic of *The Times,* she would have lived in vain. Hence the title of her autobiography. 146, 148, 165

**Orleans, Charlotte Elizabeth, Duchess of** (1652-1772). Daughter of the Elector Palatine. 198

**Ossoli, Margaret Fuller (1810-50).** American critic and social reformer; married the Marquis Angelo Ossoli in 1847. They were drowned with their child in a shipwreck when returning to the USA. 29

**Ouida,** pen-name of **Louise Ramée** (1839-1908). Flamboyant and eccentric Englishwoman who wrote unreal novels about a way of life she had never experienced. 'Her conversation was disappointing, her opinions prejudiced and her temperament extremely cynical.' She pretended that her name was de la Ramée. 116

# P

**Pankhurst, Emmeline (1858-1928).** Aggressive woman suffragist; mother of Christabel P. 177

**Parker, Dorothy (1893-1967).** Celebrated American wit, once described by Alexander Woollcott as 'so odd a blend of Little Nell and Lady Macbeth'. 39, 76, 87, 94, 96, 150, 166, 168, 217

**Parker, Suzy** 114

**Perry, Nora (1832-96).** American writer of sickening sentimentality. 36

**Peterson, Virgilia.** 100, 122

**Phelps, Elizabeth Stuart (1844-1911).** American writer; author of *The Gates Ajar.* 214

**Piatt, Sarah Morgan Bryan** (1836-1919). American poet descended from Daniel Boone. 115

**Pitter, Ruth (b. 1897).** English poet; Heinemann Foundation Award 1954; Queen's Medal for Poetry 1955. 141, 216

**Potter, Beatrix (1866-1943).** English writer and illustrator of inimitable stories for children. 30, 101, 111, 112

**Pym, Barbara (d.1980).** English novelist regarded by Lord David Cecil, Philip Larkin and many others as one of the most underrated novelists of the twentieth century. 78, 92, 165

# R

**Raverat, Gwen (1885-1957).** Granddaughter of Charles Darwin. 24, 32, 113, 121

**Repplier, Agnes (1855-1950).** American essayist of German descent; a witty, sharp and vigorous writer. 160

**Rohde, Eleanour Sinclair.** American writer of gardening books. 138

**Ros, Amanda McKittrick (1860-1939).** Irish novelist and poet, often described as Ireland's answer to William McGonagall. Her two volumes of collected poems are entitled *Fumes of Formation* and *Bayonets of Bastard Sheen.* 46, 72, 79, 146, 216

**Rossetti, Christina (1830-94)** 70, 152, 212

**Rowland, Helen (1875-1950).** American author and journalist. 39, 40, 45, 52, 54, 55, 57, 76, 77, 95, 99

# S

**Sabin, Mrs Charles H.** Played a prominent role in the campaign for the repeal of the Eighteenth Amendment. 107

**Sackville-West, Vita (1892-1962).** English poet, novelist, biographer and gardener. Married to Harold Nicolson. Her private life has recently suffered

from over-exposure. 20, 139, 140, 165
**Sappho (fl. c. 600 BC).** Greek lyric poet; the sapphic metre is named after her. 71
**Savage, Eliza Mary Ann (1836-85).** Friend of Samuel Butler; appears in *The Way of All Flesh* as Alethea; see *Letters between Samuel Butler and Miss Eliza Mary Ann Savage* (Jonathan Cape, 1935). 193
**Sayers, Dorothy L. (1893-1957).** 'Once a first-rate detective story writer who later became an exceedingly snobbish popular novelist.' 187, 215
**Schreiner, Olive (1855-1920).** South African novelist; *The Story of an African Farm,* published in 1883, caused an outcry on account of its outspoken criticism of Christianity and advocacy of the social and economic emancipation of women. 177
**Scott, Martha** 111
**Scovell, E. J. (b. 1907).** Poet; published works include *Shadows of Chrysanthemums* and *The Midsummer Meadow.* 47, 130
**Sévigné, Mme de (1626-96).** French writer and lady of fashion, famous for the letters she wrote to her daughter, the Comtesse de Grignan. 63, 211
**Sheridan, Clare (b. 1885).** English novelist and journalist; first cousin of Winston Churchill. Her brother Hugh had two sons whom he christened Saxon and Viking. 123
**Signoret, Simone (b. 1921).** French film actress, married to Yves Montand. 54
**Sitwell, Edith (1887-1964).** English self-publicist and *soi-disant* poet. 93, 158, 163
**Skinner, Cornelia Otis (b. 1910).** American actress, monologuist, playwright and essayist. 123, 158, 179
**Smart, Elizabeth.** English poet, once married to George Barker. 76, 77
**Smith, Lillian (1897-1966).** American novelist, author of *Strange Fruit* (pub. 1944), a then highly controversial story about the love of a negro girl and a white man. 144
**Smith, Stevie (1902-71).** English poetess who became widely known by reciting and singing her poems on the wireless. 46, 61, 63, 64, 114, 155, 199, 213, 217
**Smyth, Dame Ethel (1858-1944).** English composer, writer and militant suffragist; composed 'The March of the Women', battle song of the Women's Social and Political Union. 159, 185, 192, 205
**Spark, Muriel.** English novelist; became a Roman Catholic in 1954. 191

**Sproat, Nancy Dennis (1766-1827).** American writer of verse for children. 23
**Staël, Mme de (1766-1817).** French writer; born Anne Necker. She fled from France during the Revolution, was exiled by Napoleon, and only returned after the fall of the Empire in 1815. 41, 51, 113
**Stannard, Henrietta Eliza Vaughan (1856-1911).** English novelist who wrote under the pseudonym of John Strange Winter; author of such perky romantic tales as *That Imp!* and *That Miss Smith!*; also wrote numerous military romances with titles such as *In Quarters, Cavalry Life* and *A Born Soldier.* 148
**Stanton, Elizabeth Cady (1815-1902).** American women's rights leader; organised first woman's rights convention, Seneca Falls, N.Y., 1848. 178
**Stark, Freya.** Author of many travel books, mainly about the Middle East; married to Stewart Perowne, the historian. 24, 92, 180
**Stein, Gertrude (1874-1946).** American writer long resident in France; Sinclair Lewis said the question always had been: Was Miss Stein crazy, was she joking, or was she contributing 'new rhythms to an outworn English style'? His final conclusion was that she was conducting a racket. 97, 99, 123, 199, 200
**Stokes, Rose Pastor (1879-1933).** American social worker of Russian-Jewish extraction. 45
**Stowe, Harriet Beecher (1811-96).** American novelist and devoted anti-slavery compaigner. 18, 28, 161
**Streisand, Barbra (b. 1942).** American singer and actress; star of *Funny Girl.* 100

# T

**Tarbell, Ida M. (1857-1944).** American journalist and biographer. Her reputation rests on her *History of the Standard Oil Company,* a powerful indictment of that firm's early business methods. 51
**Taylor, Ann (1782-1866)** and **Jane (1783-1824).** Writers of poetry for children; Jane wrote 'I Love Little Pussy' and 'Twinkle, Twinkle, Little Star'. 145, 210
**Taylor, Elizabeth (b. 1932).** Film actress addicted to marriage and divorce. 96
**Taylor, Elizabeth (d. 1978).** English novelist of great talent. 19, 24, 165,

176, 181

Teasdale, Sara 36

Thatcher, Margaret (b. 1925). Prime Minister of Great Britain. 195

Thomas, Carey (1857-1935). American educator and feminist; long-time (1894-1922) president of Bryn Mawr College. 174

Thomas, Louisa Carroll. American writer. 107

Thompson, Flora (1877-1948). English novelist remembered for her masterly portrayal of rural life. 22, 146

Trevor, Clare 71

Turnbull, Margaret (d. 1942). Born in Glasgow, but emigrated to USA aged two; wrote many novels, plays and the scripts for a number of films. 18

Tynan, Katharine (1861-1931). Irish religious poet, popular novelist and prominent figure in the Irish 'renaissance' movement. 138, 183

# V

Vaughan, Hilda (b. 1892). Welsh novelist and widow of Charles Morgan; her short novel, *A Thing of Nought,* is a masterpiece. 134

Victoria, Queen (1819-1901). 23, 191

Viorst, Judith. American poet; married to Milton Viorst, political writer. 58, 73

# W

Walker, Mary Edwards (1832-1919). American physician and advocate of women's rights; she always wore trousers and in 1897 founded a colony for women only called 'Adamless Eden'. Died unmarried! 94

Ward, Mrs Humphry (1851-1920). Granddaughter of Dr Arnold of Rugby, niece of Matthew Arnold, mother-in-law of G. M. Trevelyan and aunt of Julian and Aldous Huxley. Copies of her best known work, *Robert Elsmere,* were given away in the USA as premiums with a bar of soap. It was said of her novels that they bore the same relationship to great fiction as atlases bear to great paintings. 151, 168

Warner, Marina (b. 1946). English writer; was married to William Shawcross, journalist. Her grandfather, Sir Pelham Warner, was keen on cricket. 50, 172

Warner, Sylvia Townsend (1893-1978). English writer and authority on cookery, wines and herbs—the last appropriate

to one so preoccupied with witchcraft. 51, 187, 206

Warrender, Lady Maud (1870-1945). Energetic do-gooder and *grande dame.* 124, 125, 185, 197

Webb, Mary (1881-1927). English novelist. 53, 129, 137, 153

Weldon, Fay (b. 1932). Trendy intellectual novelist and playwright; wrote the advertising slogan 'Go to work on an egg'. 64

Wells, Carolyn (1870-1942). Author of over 170 books, of which *The Nonsense Anthology* was the best known. 78, 104, 130, 166

West, Rebecca (b. 1892). *Née* Cecily Fairfield; her pseudonym is taken from Ibsen's *Rosmersholm.* 120

Wharton, Edith (1862-1937). American novelist and short-story writer. 157, 215

Whitehorn, Katharine. English journalist; writes an extremely witty column in *The Observer.* 41, 66, 129, 148, 199

Whitmell, Lucy (d. 1917). 184

Wickham, Anna (b.1884). British poet whose neglect by the critics is one of the mysteries of contemporary literature. 38, 63

Wilcox, Ella Wheeler (1850-1919). American poet and journalist. Author of *Poems of Passion,* which was rejected on the grounds that it was immoral. This story appeared in the newspapers and assured the book a wide sale when it eventually appeared in 1883. During 1918 she toured the army camps in France, delivering talks on sexual problems. As a result of overexertion she fell ill in the spring of 1919 and died. 145, 155, 207

Williams, Shirley (b. 1930). Labour politician; Secretary of State for Education and Science (1976-9), daughter of Vera Brittain. 18

Wilson, Barbara (1880-1943). Author of two enchanting books of memoirs; daughter of Lord Ribblesdale and mother of Peter Wilson of Sotheby's. 38

Winchilsea, Anne Finch, Countess of (1666-1720). English poet and friend of Alexander Pope, who cribbed some of her lines. 136

Windsor, Duchess of 192

Winslow, Thyra Samter (1903-1961). American writer of books, films and TV plays. 81

Winspear, Violet. English romantic novelist whose books include *Dearest Demon, Devil's Darling* and *Dangerous*

*Delight.* 76

**Woolf, Virginia (1882-1941).** English novelist and co-founder in 1917 with her husband Leonard of The Hogarth Press; the focal member of the Bloomsbury Group. 47, 104, 107, 128, 176, 179, 186

**Wordsworth, Dorothy (1771-1855).** Only sister of, and housekeeper to, William W., who did acknowledge how much he owed to her inspiring companionship. In 1829 she suffered a nervous breakdown from which she never recovered. 136, 137

**Wylie, Elinor (1885-1928).** American novelist. 'She looked like a white queen of a white country.' 153, 154

# Z

**Zogbaum, Mrs Harry St Clair (1881-1941).** 91

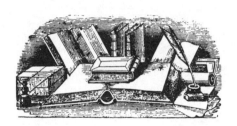

RECEIVED
NOV 1982
Mission College
Learning Resource
Services